Mitra Mann is a specialist private client litigator in contentious probate and Court of Protection matters. She deals with cases involving wills and inheritance disputes, executor and trustee removal, restoring a vulnerable person's estate in the High Court and a range of Court of Protection applications.

Mitra is particularly passionate about protecting vulnerable adults. She is a trained Dementia Friends Champion dedicated to raising awareness of mental capacity issues locally and nationally. One way of preventing financial abuse, whether done intentionally or unintentionally, is to share information with other professionals, carers, financial advisers, attorneys and deputies. To this end, Mitra published her first book in 2024: "Court of Protection – a Practical Guide to Gifting". She has also written articles and delivered webinars and seminars in several Court of Protection practice areas.

Financial Abuse: A Practical Guide to Removing Attorneys and Deputies

A Guide for Practitioners, Attorneys and Deputies

Financial Abuse: A Practical Guide to Removing Attorneys and Deputies

A Guide for Practitioners, Attorneys and Deputies

Mitra Mann LLB (Hons)
PGDip in Legal Practice
PGCert in Medical Law and Ethics

Law Brief Publishing

Published 2026 by Law Brief Publishing, an imprint of Law Brief Publishing Ltd
30 The Parks
Minehead
Somerset
TA24 8BT

www.lawbriefpublishing.com

Paperback: 978-1-918241-06-8

To my mother-in-law, Sylvia Boyce,
a fellow lawyer who shared her wisdom with me.

To Daniel Boyce, Deep Mann and Oliver Boyce-Mann –
thank you for your continued support.

PREFACE

The purpose of this book is primarily to raise awareness about a growing problem which our society is facing: the abuse of vulnerable people who place their trust and confidence in those who subsequently abuse this trust. Whilst this applies to only a small percentage of the population, the increase in the number of cases recently reported, particularly concerning financial abuse, is eye-watering.

Financial abuse has placed many vulnerable people in precarious situations. It is vital that we have information on how to recognise when abuse may be happening and how to respond to it. The author's aim is to help the public understand this growing concern so that they can be vigilant and take steps to protect the vulnerable members of our society. In addition, practitioners who advise on the management of P's[1] property and affairs or deal with concerns raised in respect of an attorney's[2] or a deputy's[3] conduct may also find this guide helpful.

It should, however, be noted that not all cases of financial abuse involve "P" and their attorneys or deputies. There are cases where the victim retains the capacity to make financial decisions, and the abuser is not acting in any formal or legal capacity. In such circumstances, invoking the High Court's inherent jurisdiction will be more appropriate,

---

1 For the purposes of this book, "P" is defined as someone who lacks the capacity to make certain decisions in respect of their property and finances.

2 For the purposes of this book, an attorney is someone who has been appointed to make decisions in respect of the donor's property and affairs only (and not in respect of health and welfare matters).

3 For the purposes of this book, a deputy is someone who has been appointed by the Court of Protection to make decisions in respect of P's property and affairs only, unless otherwise specified by the author.

particularly where the risk of future possible abuse is a real possibility, and not a merely a risk.

This book deals specifically with protecting "P" – someone who has lost the capacity to make decisions regarding their finances – in circumstances where an appointed attorney or deputy breaches their fiduciary duty when managing P's property and affairs. Although there is a logical sequence to the chapters in this book, it has been written so that it can be read in any order, depending on who the reader is: whether it is a concerned friend, relative or organisation; an attorney or a deputy who wishes to understand the scope of their powers; or a practitioner navigating through the complexities of Court of Protection proceedings after financial abuse has been identified.

This book is by no means the main authority on financial abuse and how to deal with attorneys or deputies who have misused their powers. It is recommended that readers refer to other sources of information and materials including the Mental Capacity Act 2005, the Mental Capacity Act 2005 Code of Practice, the Court of Protection Rules 2017 as well as the Office of the Public Guardian's Guidance on how to be a property and finances attorney[4]; the Guidance for Professional Deputies[5] and the Public Guardian's Practice Note on agreeing to act as a professional attorney.[6]

The author has used examples from her professional experience combined with other scenarios to create fictitious case studies in this book. The author hopes that this book will make readers, including potential victims, aware of these topical issues.

Note that the case studies in this book are purely fictional.

---

4 LP14.

5 Published in February 2023and some sections are applicable to lay deputies.

6 Practice Note PN1.

The information and law quoted in this book was believed to be correct as of 30 November 2025.

Mitra Mann
January 2026

GLOSSARY

Protected person (P) – a person who lacks the capacity to make certain decisions because of an impairment of, or disturbance in the functioning of their mind or brain.

Attorney – someone who is chosen and appointed by another person (known as a donor) to make certain decisions on their behalf.

Code of Practice – guidance which supports the Mental Capacity Act 2005 and explains how this legislation should be interpreted and implemented when making decisions on behalf of P.

Court of Protection (COP) – a specialist Court established in 2007 which makes specific decisions on behalf of or relating to P; or appoints other people known as deputies to make decisions on behalf of P.

Mental Capacity Act 2005 (MCA 2005) – legislation which came into effect on 1 October 2007 making provisions relating to and to protect those who lack the capacity to make decisions (P).

Office of the Public Guardian (OPG) – a government body, working within the framework of the Mental Capacity Act 2005, that maintains a register of attorneys, deputies and guardians. Part of the Public Guardian's role involves supporting and supervising attorneys and deputies; investigating concerns regarding their actions; and taking steps deemed necessary to protect P's interests.

Official Solicitor (OS) – part of the Ministry of Justice acting for those who are unable to represent themselves in court proceedings. The OS would normally be appointed if P does not have a litigation friend or there is not anyone suitable to represent P's interests in a court case.

CONTENTS

CHAPTER ONE

FINANCIAL ABUSE

1.1 – Financial abuse: a growing concern

It is a sad fact of life that financial abuse is on the rise. In her first book on the topic of gifts made by attorneys and deputies,[1] the author identified this growing concern and anticipated there would be more cases of financial abuse making the headlines following the difficult economic and financial circumstances experienced by many during the Covid-19 pandemic. During this unprecedented period, and following social isolation imposed by the government, many vulnerable people found themselves detached from the outer world and their loved ones. There were fewer frank and open conversations, and it is not surprising that many unlawful actions went unnoticed at the time.

A report identifying these issues was published in February 2024 by STEP[2] together with the Alzheimer's Society: "Loss of Mental Capacity: A Global Perspective".[3] One of the key findings of the survey was "*Financial abuse is increasing. It is most prevalent when there is uncertainty about whether a person lacks the mental capacity to make a decision or when a representative is exercising their authority on behalf of the uncapable person.*"[4]

1 Published in March 2024: https://www.lawbriefpublishing.com/CourtofProtectionGifting/.

2 STEP is a global professional body comprising lawyers, accountants and other professionals who help families plan for the future.

3 This report was published together with the Alzheimer's Society and a copy can be downloaded by accessing the following link: http://step.org/research-reports/mental-capacity.

4 Page 7 of the Loss of Mental Capacity: A Global Perspective report.

Recent headlines in 2024 and 2025 have also highlighted the fact that financial abuse is a known problem and on the increase. In February 2024, Lancs Live reported that Rachel Dawes was sentenced to two and a half years in prison.[5] Rachel Dawes was a carer who looked after a 60-year-old man who had learning difficulties. She was found to have stolen in excess of £30,000 from him over a period of three and half years (which included the period when the Covid-19 pandemic was rife). Rachel Dawes had access to and used the vulnerable person's bank account to shop on Amazon Prime and eBay; purchase jewellery and take aways; and on betting. She also used his bank account to make several other payments. As a result, the vulnerable person she was meant to be caring for was left with a minimal amount of around £65.00 in his bank account. He could not afford food or other basic utilities, leaving him in precarious circumstances. Another carer subsequently discovered the problem when she noted irregular payments in the bank statements. This was investigated by the police, and the matter went to trial in the Liverpool Crown Court where subsequently, Rachel Dawes was found guilty and was sentenced to prison.

A few months later, in August 2024, another case was heard in the Swindon Crown Court and BBC News, Wiltshire reported that David Eggleton was sentenced to prison for five and a half years for misappropriating around £600,000 from his elderly aunt between 2018 and 2020.[6] In this case, David Eggleton acted in his capacity as an attorney for financial affairs, having been appointed as such by his aunt in 2017. Following his appointment, David Eggleton took advantage of his position and transferred large sums of his aunt's money into his personal bank account. He used the funds for his own benefit which included purchasing cars, paying for holidays and paying off his

5 'Despicable' carer stole £30k from disabled man to fund Netflix and takeaways – LancsLive, by Wesley Homes and Jon Macpherson, 28 Feb 2024

6 Wiltshire man jailed for stealing £600k through power of attorney – BBC News by Bea Swallow, 1 August 2024

mortgage. In this case, the aunt who still had the capacity to make decisions regarding her financial affairs, raised concerns when she became aware that her care home fees were not being paid, and revoked the power of attorney. The police launched an investigation and the Crown Prosecution Service subsequently prosecuted David Eggleton.

In the same month (August 2024), another case was heard in the Manchester Crown Court and was reported by The Mail on Sunday.[7] In this case, the vulnerable person had appointed a minister at her church, Paul Flowers, as her attorney for property and affairs. She placed her trust in a "man of cloth" and believed that he would manage her financial affairs sensibly given that he had experience working in the banking and finance sectors. However, Paul Flowers used his position to benefit himself. The vulnerable person's monies were used to fund his personal and expensive habits. He withdrew around £70,0000 from her bank account and purchased alcohol from The Wine Society, paid for holidays and cruises abroad and spent monies on other luxurious items, none of which was for the vulnerable person's benefit. The police launched an investigation and Paul Flowers subsequently admitted to acting fraudulently and pleaded guilty.

What is notable in the above cases is that the abuse was committed by someone who had no familial links to the vulnerable person. Sadly, family members are not immune to temptation and have been known to misuse their powers. In March 2025, BBC News reported that John Wilcox's granddaughter, Amy (daughter of his stepson), had accepted a police caution for fraud for misappropriating funds from John Wilcox's bank account.[8] It was reported that after being diagnosed with dementia, John Wilcox became delusional and paranoid, particularly after he was

---

7 'Crystal Methodist' former Co-op bank boss Paul Flowers facing jail over £100,000 friend swindle | Daily Mail Online by Lix Hull, Northern Correspondent, 25 July 2024

8 Isolated and confused: How a granddad 'vanished' from his family – BBC News by Sue Mitchell and Ben Milne, 29 March 2025

hospitalised during Covid when restrictions on social interaction were in place, and he could not have visitors. He felt isolated and allowed Amy to take charge by appointing her as his attorney under a Lasting Power of Attorney instrument. Unfortunately for John Wilcox, the decision to give her control resulted in him being found in a hotel room, dishevelled, living in appalling conditions with no cleaning services or food and with only 16p in his bank account.

As seen in the above-mentioned cases, the Crown Prosecution Service will prosecute attorneys following investigations carried out by the police. The Fraud Act 2006 enables the police to take action in serious cases of abuse. As part of their investigation, the police will interview the attorney, the deputy or anyone in a position of trust. If there is sufficient evidence that the person concerned committed fraud and depending on the level of abuse which has taken place or is about to take place, they will refer the matter to the Crown Prosecution Service.

However, in reality, only a few cases are prosecuted by the Crown Prosecution Service. This may be for several reasons such as the inability of the victim to give a clear statement; or the victim refusing to give evidence for fear of being abandoned; or the perpetrator using legal loopholes and claiming that that the "gifts" were made voluntarily and at a time when P had capacity.

The author interviewed Paul Smith,[9] who worked for the police force as a vulnerable adult investigative co-ordinator and his role included putting together procedures to protect vulnerable people. In his view, there are not many detectives allocated to this field, and cases of this nature are dealt with mainly by police officers in uniform who very often write off the financial case as a civil matter. According to him, the main barriers to the police investigating financial abuse cases include:

[9] Paul Smith is now a financial crime specialist with over 30 years of experience in this field.

- A lack of training and understanding within the police force.
- The victim having fluctuating capacity.
- A lack of consent from the victim to take the case further.

So, what happens in cases where there is some evidence of misappropriation of assets but which the police cannot or will not take further? In such circumstances, the civil courts can help. There are other means to stop financial abuse and bring justice to a victim. This book addresses the other options which can be considered, particularly when an attorney or a deputy breaches their duties and misuses their powers.[10]

1.2 – Attorney and deputy misconduct: the statistics

In many cases involving financial abuse, the perpetrator is often the person who has been trusted to manage the victim's finances. They are given the legal authority to access P's property and finances by way of a power of attorney instrument or a deputyship order.

It is noted from some cases that it was the attorney's or deputy's intention from the very start to deprive P of their assets for their own personal gain. They were fully aware that their actions were fraudulent and unlawful. However, there are also many cases where an attorney or a deputy made unlawful decisions because of a lack of understanding of the scope of their powers in that particular capacity. This issue was highlighted in the report published by STEP in February 2024: "*It's a good thing that the donor gets to choose their own attorney. However, they don't always make the best choices. Education of the representatives (in respect of their role and authority) is lacking.*"[11]

---

10 See Chapter 5 of this book.

11 STEP report on "Loss of Mental Capacity: A Global Perspective", page 24.

Drawing from the author's own experience as well as the cases heard in the Court of Protection, there appear to be 2 main misconceptions which tend to influence an attorney's or a deputy's action:

1) They believe they can do whatever they like with P's monies and assets once they are appointed.

2) They believe that P could or would have allowed them to take these actions if only they had capacity.

The author has had conversations with lay attorneys and deputies in charge of managing P's finances. When faced with a potential decision which involves parting with P's assets, their understanding of their role is alarming. The author referred to a few statements made by attorneys and deputies in her first book[12] and repeats them in this section since readers are likely to relate to them:

- *"[P] had capacity and said that I could have the money."*
- *"[P] would have wanted me to have the money if only they had capacity."*
- *"It will all be mine soon anyway, so what is the problem?"*
- *"I deserve this, for all the sacrifice I am making."*
- *"I will return the money, if [P] ever has a need for it."*
- *"If [P] does not mind and is well cared for, what is the harm?"*

Misconceptions such as these often lead to financial abuse, and it comes as no surprise that the number of complaints made to the Office of the

12 Court of Protection: A Practical Guide to Gifting, Chapter 5, para 5.1.

Public Guardian[13] has risen over the past few years. A large number of these complaints is in relation to an attorney's or a deputy's conduct regarding their management of P's financial affairs.

To put matters into context, in 2018/2019, the Office of the Public Guardian carried out 2,883 investigations. This increased to 3,099 in 2019/2020. There was a decline in the number of investigations carried out in 2020/2021, mainly due to the Office of the Public Guardian not being able to accept cases for investigation during the pandemic when the risk of spreading the coronavirus disease was very high. With the easing of rules on social distancing post-pandemic, complaints and investigations are once again on the rise. The investigations accepted by the Office of the Public Guardian increased from 2,089 to 2,464 in 2021/2022;[14] from 2,464 to 2,849 in 2022/2023;[15] from 2,849 to 3,647 in 2023/2024;[16] and further increased from 3,647 to 3,823 in 2024/2025.[17]

1.3 – Spotting the signs of financial abuse

It is often thought that abuse takes place "behind closed doors" and is therefore difficult to identify. Whilst this may be true in some circumstances, there are often telltale signs which indicate that someone

13 The Office of the Guardian (OPG) was established in 2007 to safeguard the interests of P and supervise deputies. Part of their role involves carrying out investigations where there are safeguarding issues and/or financial abuse concerns relating to deputies and registered attorneys.

14 https://www.gov.uk/government/publications/opg-annual-report-and-accounts-2021-to-2022/opg-annual-report-and-accounts-2021-to-2022

15 https://www.gov.uk/government/publications/office-of-the-public-guardian-annual-report-2022-to-2023

16 https://assets.publishing.service.gov.uk/media/66a1092ffc8e12ac3edb03ff/opg-annual-report-and-accounts-2023-to-2024.pdf

17 https://www.gov.uk/government/publications/opg-annual-report-and-accounts-2024-to-2025

may be taking advantage of P's vulnerability. It is vital that the public is better informed of these signs.

Those who are involved in P's care and the management of their affairs – for instance family members, close friends, carers, the banks where P holds their accounts, the local authority, care homes, etc – are likely to be the first ones to identify a potential mismanagement of P's financial affairs by their attorney or deputy.

The author lists below a few of these telltale signs and encourages readers to be vigilant and look out for them:[18]

- Large or frequent withdrawals from P's bank account through the ATM.
- Adding someone else's name to P's bank account, without specifying they are P's attorney or deputy.
- Signatures on cheques that do not match.
- Applying for credit in P's name.
- Missing jewellery or other valuables.
- Non-payment of P's regular outgoings or utility bills resulting in lack of adequate food, heating or clothing.
- Non-payment of P's care home fees.
- Unexpected changes to P's Will.

[18] The author recommends visiting https://www.step.org/mental-capacity/spot-the-signs

- P deferring to someone else to answer for them.
- P looking dishevelled, unkempt and malnourished.
- Controlling or restricting P's personal contact with others by turning visitors away.
- Controlling or restricting P's communications with others by denying P of their telephone and/or not allowing them to answer calls.

Financial abuse can also be subtle, such as the purchase of a car when P is no longer able to drive or the purchase of a lawnmower when P does not have a garden to tend to.

Concerns of this nature can be emotionally charged, and it is not uncommon for practitioners to receive enquiries from potential clients asking whether they can "take someone to court". Whilst court proceedings may be an option, other avenues should be explored in the first instance. In Chapter 5 of this book, the author lists other courses of action which should be considered before escalating matters to the Court of Protection or the High Court.

Author's Note: Is financial abuse a rising concern which our society is facing? Or has it always been a problem but previously went undetected due to limited awareness and available resources? It is the author's view that financial abuse is not a novel problem. Recent factors such as an increase in wealth; an ageing population; more awareness through social media; legal responsibilities placed on organisations such as the Office of the Public Guardian, the police, and the Local Authority, have led to more cases being detected at an early stage.

1.4 – Case Study: Rohan

Rohan is a 76-year-old widower. He was married to Uma, and they had a daughter – Anita. Ten years ago, Rohan and Uma instructed solicitors to make their Wills and a Lasting Power of Attorney in respect of their finances. Their wishes were simple and straightforward: they wished to leave their estate to each other with the provision that Anita would be the sole beneficiary upon the death of the surviving parent. Wills were made to this effect. They also appointed each other and Anita as their attorneys on a joint and several basis. Their Property and Affairs Lasting Power of Attorney was registered with the Office of the Public Guardian.

Rohan and Uma had been married for 45 years when Uma died of a heart attack 2 years ago. Her death was sudden and took Rohan and Anita by surprise. After Uma's death, Rohan became withdrawn and lost interest in a lot of things, including his finances. With Uma gone, Rohan turned to Anita for assistance and company.

Anita initially set up Rohan's finances in such a way that Rohan would be able to manage effortlessly. She made sure that all utility bills were paid by direct debit from Rohan's current account, which Rohan had access to. Rohan's pension easily covered his monthly outgoings. He also had savings of £120,000 and these funds were transferred in a separate bank account for a rainy day – an account which Anita managed in her capacity as Rohan's attorney.[19] Rohan only sought Anita's input if any major decisions had to be made.

Last year, Rohan started showing signs of confusion and forgetfulness. He would leave the front door open overnight; forget to cook and/or eat for a couple of days. Anita arranged for Rohan to see his GP and

---

19 Since Rohan's Lasting Power of Attorney (LPA) appointed Rita and Anita jointly and severally, the LPA instrument was still valid after Uma's death and Anita could continue acting as Rohan's attorney.

Rohan was subsequently diagnosed with vascular dementia. It became clear that Rohan could no longer make certain financial decisions and needed assistance if he were to remain living at home on his own.

Anita engaged the services of a care agency, and a carer named Seema became Rohan's main carer. The arrangement was that Anita would visit Rohan at the weekends; do the grocery shopping; and keep the fridge well stocked. Seema would visit Rohan on Mondays, Wednesdays and Fridays; cook for Rohan on those days and provide him with personal care.

The arrangement worked well for the first 3-4 months. However, soon after, Seema found Rohan in soiled clothing on a Monday morning. Rohan informed Seema that he had not eaten, and Seema noted that the fridge was not stocked. Seema telephoned Anita but was unable to reach her. When she finally managed to speak to Anita, Anita was evasive and explained that she had been on a cruise with her friends. Seema asked if there were other relatives or friends whom she could contact in the event Anita was not available. Anita was clear that no one else but her should visit or get involved in her father's care. Anita promised to purchase grocery items the next day, a promise she never kept.

This became a regular pattern and started having a detrimental effect on Rohan. Rohan was not set up for online banking. Even though he had access to his bank card, he no longer remembered his pin number to withdraw cash from the ATM. Anita refused to provide Seema or the care agency with funds to purchase food items for Rohan when this was requested. At times, Anita also forgot to pay the care agency's invoices. On recent occasions when Anita visited Rohan during the week – predominantly to intercept and collect the post – Seema noticed that she drove a brand-new Jaguar and carried an expensive designer handbag.

Seema became increasingly concerned. On one of her visits, she found Rohan upset after he had opened his post. Rohan was confused. He did not know what to do and asked Seema to check the papers. Seema looked at a couple of bank statements which showed multiple online purchases from Amazon as well as a large payment in the sum of £7,500 made to P&O Cruises a few months ago. Rohan's current account was overdrawn, and his savings account now showed a balance of only £15,000. The other letters suggested there were several overdue electricity and water bills.

Spotting the signs:

The author has presented a basic case study and acknowledges that other cases may involve greater complexity. However, the purpose of this exercise is to bring to the reader's attention to typical signs which would often trigger alarm bells for carers, family members, neighbours, friends, co-attorneys, etc.

In this case study, the telltale signs which would cause Seema to be concerned include:

- Non-payment of regular utility bills and the care agency's invoices, suggesting mismanagement and/or insufficient funds in Rohan's bank account.

- Not purchasing food and other basic items for Rohan's use.

- A payment in the sum of £7,500 made to a travel agency when Rohan had not been away and there were no upcoming holidays planned for him.

- Unusual online expenses, particularly when Rohan is not set up for online banking and items had not been delivered to his home for his use.

- A significant drop in Rohan's savings which has not been accounted for.

- A notable upgrade in Anita's lifestyle.

- Anita's evasiveness when being asked simple questions relating to Rohan's wellbeing.

- Controlling and limiting Rohan's contact with others.

What can be done?

Where a vulnerable person like Rohan is at risk, immediate steps should be taken to (i) safeguard Rohan; and (ii) try and prevent further potential financial abuse from taking place. The author addresses this in Chapter 5 of this book.

CHAPTER TWO

CREATING A VALID LPA – THE IMPORTANCE OF A SUITABLE ATTORNEY AND CERTIFICATE PROVIDER

There are several types of power of attorney instruments – a General or Ordinary Power of Attorney; an Enduring Power of Attorney; and a Lasting Power of Attorney. There is a common misconception that a next of kin has powers similar to an attorney. This is not the case. A next of kin does not have any specific legal rights. By creating a power of attorney instrument, the donor has the assurance that their choice will be respected, and the appointed attorney(s) are given the certainty that they have the legal authority to make certain decisions on behalf of the donor.

In this book, the author focuses specifically on Property and Affairs Lasting Powers of Attorney instruments and will refer to them as an "LPA instrument" or "LPA". The aim of this chapter is to highlight the importance of appointing the most suitable attorney and having an appropriate certificate provider confirm that the donor is making the LPA instrument of their own free will and that they understand its implications. From experience, if these prerequisites are not met it can lead to a potential objection to the registration of the LPA instrument or the revocation of a registered power of attorney instrument – which the author addresses in Chapters 4 and 6 of this book.

2.1 – Identifying a suitable attorney

The powers of an attorney are usually defined in the power of attorney instrument. They can be wide, and this is why it is crucial that the donor appoints the right attorney(s). The following key factors should be considered by the donor when identifying a prospective attorney:[20]

- The attorney must be aged over 18.
- The attorney is not bankrupt or subject to a debt relief order.
- It is advisable for the attorney to be reasonably financially astute and have experience in successfully managing their own affairs.
- Ideally, the attorney should have knowledge of the way the donor has managed their finances in the past and what the donor's future plans are, including their testamentary wishes.
- If the donor is appointing more than one attorney, whether the attorneys will be able to work harmoniously.

> Author's note: The author has come across many cases where donor parents appointed all their children as attorneys so as not to upset any of them. This is despite being aware that the children do not get on with one another or have had personal financial difficulties.
>
> It is recognised that maintaining family harmony is an important part of life. However, donors should be advised to be pragmatic and focus on who is most appropriate to handle their finances. If the donor feels that their choice of attorneys will cause a rift in the family or is suspicious of one of the intended attorneys, making an LPA instrument at this point may not be in their best interests. Other options may include appointing a neutral lay or professional attorney(s) or leaving it to the Court of Protection to appoint a deputy in the future, if required. From experience, appointing attorneys who

[20] This is not an exhaustive list, and other factors should be considered depending on the circumstances and the value of the donor's assets.

cannot work harmoniously very often leads to suspicion (whether substantiated or not) and potential contested applications made to the Court of Protection for the removal of certain attorney(s).

2.2 – What are the attorney's responsibilities?

The responsibilities of an attorney are multifaceted but the key message to any attorney is that they must always make decisions which are in the donor's best interests and be mindful of the checklist in section 4 of the Mental Capacity Act 2005.

The general duties of a property and affairs attorney include:[21]

- Applying certain standards of care and skill (duty of care) when making decisions.
- Carrying out the donor's instructions.
- Not taking advantage of their position and not benefitting themselves but benefit the donor (fiduciary duty).
- Not delegating decisions, unless authorised to do so.
- Acting in good faith.
- Respecting confidentiality.
- Complying with the directions of the Court of Protection.
- Not giving up the role without telling the donor and the court.

21 Mental Capacity Act 2005, Code of Practice, para 7.58

- Keeping accounts and the donor's money and property separate from their own.

In terms of the actions which a Property and Affairs attorney can take or decisions which they can make on behalf of the donor, these are set out clearly in the Code of Practice and include:[22]

- Buying or selling the donor's property.
- Opening, closing or operating any bank, building society or other account.
- Giving access to the donor's financial information.
- Claiming, receiving and using (on the donor's behalf) all benefits, pensions, allowances and rebates.
- Receiving any income, inheritance or other entitlement on behalf of the donor.
- Dealing with the donor's tax affairs.
- Paying the donor's mortgage, rent and household expenses.
- Insuring, maintaining and repairing the donor's property.
- Investing the donor's savings.
- Making limited gifts on the donor's behalf.[23]

---

[22] Mental Capacity Act 2005, Code of Practice, para 7.36

[23] For further information of the scope of their powers, see section 12(2) of the Mental Capacity Act 2005. Also refer to the author's first book – Court of Protection: A Practical Guide to Gifting.

- Paying for private medical care and residential care or nursing home fees.

- Applying for any entitlement to funding for NHS care, social care or adaptations.

- Using the donor's money to buy a vehicle or any equipment or other help they need.

- Repaying interest and capital on any loan taken out by the donor.

Whilst at first glance, managing someone else's affairs may not seem complex since most attorneys already make such decisions in their personal life, in reality, it is often difficult for an attorney to separate their personal feelings and views from what is in the donor's or P's best interests, particularly in a familial setting. In Chapter 1.2 of this book, the author mentions 2 main common misconceptions which attorneys often adopt when making decisions on behalf of P. In the next sub-chapter, the author identifies the main root of these misconceptions and what can be done to help attorneys have a better understanding of their role and the scope of their powers.

2.3 – Who advises the attorney?

There appears to be a gap in the LPA-making process. Professionals (if instructed) will usually advise donors on the implications of making an LPA instrument and what the attorney(s) can and cannot do. However, such detailed advice is not usually given to the intended attorney(s) as it is often not part of the professional person's retainer with the donor. Intended attorneys are often sent the LPA instrument signed by the donor and are advised to refer to the Mental Capacity Act 2005, Code of Conduct before they sign the LPA instrument. However, how many attorneys will read the Code of Practice (which is around 300 pages long) before agreeing to act and signing the LPA instrument? It is the author's view that this lack of advice to attorneys from the very outset has contributed to the growing number of cases of attorneys misusing their powers.

It is therefore important for attorneys to (i) be provided with sufficient advice at the time they agree to become an attorney; and (ii) this advice and access to information should continue to be provided to them after their appointment and the LPA instrument is registered with the Office of the Public Guardian. The author is an advocate for attorneys (and deputies) having access to legal advice, training and guidance from very early on. This will help them navigate through complex situations; make informed decisions; and ensure they remain transparent and accountable at every stage.[24]

The Mental Capacity Act 2005 Code of Practice[25] is a good starting point for attorneys. It explains how the Mental Capacity Act 2005 operates on a day-to-day basis and offers examples and case scenarios to guide attorneys when making decisions and/or when in doubt. In addition, various other organisations and professionals have published detailed guidance and articles to assist attorneys and deputies.

2.4 – Case Study: Julianne – Considering financial implications pre and post-death

As mentioned in Chapter 2.1 of this book, it is important for the chosen attorney[26] to have some knowledge of how the donor managed their finances in the past and what their testamentary wishes are. When making financial decisions, careful consideration should be given by the attorney as to how their actions are likely to have an impact on the donor's current and future financial situation as well as the impact post-death. An attorney should try and avoid frustrating the donor's

[24] The author is currently working on a project to make such information and advice are accessible to attorneys and deputies.

[25] Published on 22 July 2013 and last updated on 14 October 2020

[26] This applies to a deputy appointed by the Court of Protection to manage P's property and affairs.

testamentary wishes and familiarising themselves with the contents of their Will is therefore key, as the case scenario below will highlight.[27]

> Julianne and Robert were married for several years. During their marriage, they acquired 2 properties: their family home and a rental property. They have 2 sons – John and Spencer. They treated their sons equally and were consistent with their wishes that their estate should be shared between their sons equally after their death. Both sons live abroad, having secured good jobs after completing their university studies. Although they live abroad, they regularly visit their parents with their children and the family dynamics never changed.
>
> Robert passed away 4 years ago. Julianne became the sole owner of both properties pursuant to the rules of survivorship. She saw a local solicitor to put her financial affairs in order. At the time, the family home was worth around £200,000 and the rental property was of a similar value. Julianne decided to make a Will leaving Spencer the family home; John the rental property and for the residuary estate to be distributed amongst her grandchildren. She also appointed her close friend, Samantha, as her attorney. Julianne did not want to burden her sons with this responsibility since they live abroad. Samantha has been a family friend for decades and knows John and Spencer well. Julianne specifically mentioned to Samantha that she would like to remain in the family home until her death.

---

[27] Unless there are instructions in the LPA instrument specifying that the attorney should not have access to a copy of the donor's Will, attorneys and deputies are entitled to request a copy of the Will and review its contents. See the Ethics Guidance published by the SRA "Access to and disclosure of an incapacitated person's will". If the attorney or deputy does not know the whereabouts of the Will, they can carry out a search with The National Will Register: https://www.nationalwillregister.co.uk/search-for-a-will/

> Julianne has recently been diagnosed with dementia following a long period of ill health. She is no longer able to make financial decisions and requires one to one care, 24 hours a day. Julianne's pension together with the income from the rental property are no longer sufficient to pay for her care at home. Samantha is aware of her wish to remain in the family home and decides to sell the rental property to fund Julianne's care.

Consequences of selling the rental property

If Samantha were to proceed with her decision to sell the rental property, the gift of the rental property to John will be adeemed. Assuming that the family home has not been sold by the time Julianne dies and there are some funds left from the sale proceeds of the rental property which will form part of the residuary estate, Julianne's estate will be distributed as follows:

- Robert will receive the family home.
- Julianne's grandchildren will receive the residuary estate.

John will not receive anything from Julianne's estate, not even what is left of the sale proceeds of the rental property since he is not a residuary beneficiary of the estate. This clearly would not be in line with Julianne's testamentary wishes.

The above case study is an example of how a financial decisions made during P's lifetime can have a marked impact on the future. It is important for an attorney to think ahead and consider future implications before making financial decisions on behalf of P. However, this does not mean that the attorney should put a future beneficiary's interests before P's interests. The primary obligation of an attorney is to act in the donor's best interests.

What else should Samantha consider?

In this case study, Samantha is not likely to be criticised if she decides that it is in Julianne's best interests to sell the rental property so that Julianne can remain living in the comfort of her family home for as long as she possibly can. This is in line with the wishes which Julianne expressed to Samantha at a time when she had capacity. Nonetheless, Samantha should consider what else can be done so as to not to frustrate Julianne's testamentary wishes. For instance, are there other options to fund Julianne's care at home? Is Julianne entitled to a receive a contribution towards the payment of her care from the Local Authority? If there are no other reasonable options, a sale of the rental property may be inevitable. In such circumstances, a way to try and uphold Julianne's testamentary wishes may be for Samantha to seek the Court of Protection's approval for a statutory will to be made on behalf of Julianne to ensure that John remains a beneficiary of his mother's estate.[28]

2.5 – Steps to follow when creating an LPA instrument

Once a donor has identified suitable attorney(s), the next step is to complete the LPA document and there is a strict order to follow when creating an LPA instrument:

1. The donor signs the LPA instrument first.

2. The witness signs the LPA instrument to verify the donor's signature.

3. The certificate provider then signs their section.

4. Attorney(s) and/or replacement attorney(s) sign.

[28] Statutory Will applications can be complex and expensive, and it is recommended to seek legal advice before such an application is made.

5. The witness signs to verify the attorney(s) and/or replacement attorney(s) signature.

6. The LPA instrument is then sent to the Office of the Public Guardian for registration.

As people are becoming more aware of the importance of an LPA instrument, more LPAs are being created and registered with the Office of the Public Guardian. According to the statistics published by the Office of the Public Guardian, between 2023 and 2024, they received a total of 1.37 million applications to register power of attorney instruments (to include LPAs and EPAs) compared to the 1 million applications they received in the previous year.[29]

2.5 – Creating an LPA instrument online

Whilst an LPA instrument can still be made using paper forms, the Office of the Public Guardian provides donors with an online service to make LPAs at minimal cost. This service involves the donor creating an LPA online account with the Office of the Public Guardian. The donor (or someone assisting the donor) will be asked a series of questions, and the answers are then used to create the LPA document.[30] Once the LPA document is created and the donor is satisfied with it, the donor will be required to pay the application fee,[31] print the LPA document, get everyone involved to sign it [32] before it is sent to the Office of the Public Guardian for registration.

---

29 Office of the Public Guardian annual report and accounts 2023-2024, page 9.

30 The LPA document does not need to be completed in one go. A draft will be saved, and the donor can go back to it at a later stage to answer all the questions before completing it.

31 £92 as of November 2025.

32 An LPA document will require the wet signatures of the donor, the certificate provider as well as the chosen attorneys.

Author's note: Although this is an online service, the completed LPA document still needs to be printed and signed by everyone before it is posted to the Office of the Public Guardian. The whole process cannot therefore be completed online.

This online service can be a useful tool. Whilst one does not have to use the services of a solicitor or a professional person to create an LPA instrument, if the donor is vulnerable or their financial affairs are complex, it is advisable to seek professional help to create and register an LPA instrument. Instructing a professional person will give the donor the assurance required and prevent problems at a later stage. There is benefit in obtaining tailor made advice, the main ones being:

- The professional person will take instructions directly from the donor as to their wishes. With the online application, there is a risk that someone is applying pressure on the donor to complete the LPA form, appointing them as their attorney(s).

- The donor will often be asked about their family dynamics and will be offered other options, particularly if their choice of attorneys is likely to cause problems in the future.[33]

- The donor will have the opportunity to consider whether they would wish for some people to be notified of their application to register the LPA instrument.

- The donor will have the opportunity to discuss their specific preferences and instructions to include in their LPA form and whether these are likely to be effective and registered by the Office of the Public Guardian.

[33] See Author's note in Chapter 2.1 of this book.

- The professional person is also likely to act as a certificate provider in this process.[34]

- The professional person will ensure that the LPA form has been correctly executed (and in the right order) before it is sent to the Office of the Public Guardian for registration.

2.7 – The importance of a certificate provider

Once the donor has completed the main sections of the LPA form and signed in the presence of a witness, a certificate provider is required to complete section 10 of the LPA form. Not anyone can act as a certificate provider, and readers are referred to the statement and restrictions at section 10 of an LPA form for further information. In brief, a certificate provider can be an independent person who has known the donor for more than 2 years or a professional person who has the relevant skills and expertise.

A certificate provider has an important role which includes confirming that (i) the donor understands the purpose of the instrument and the scope of the authority conferred under it; (ii) no fraud or undue pressure is being used to induce the donor to create a lasting power of attorney; and (iii) there is nothing else which would prevent a lasting power of attorney from being created by the instrument.[35] In other words, the certificate provider acts as a safeguard against potential abuse. They are also crucial in establishing the validity of the LPA instrument, if it is questioned at a later date.

Before signing the statement at section 10 of the LPA form, it is important for a certificate provider to ask relevant questions of the donor to ensure the donor fully understands the implications of the LPA

---

[34] The author addresses the importance of a certificate provider in Chapter 2.7 of this book.

[35] Mental Capacity Act 2005, Schedule 1, paragraph 2(1)(e).

instrument. Such questions should include asking the donor to describe in their own words their understanding of the following:

- What type of LPA they are making.[36]
- Who they have appointed as their attorney(s) and their reasons for doing so.
- On what basis they have appointed their attorneys (if more than one) and the difference between a joint appointment and a joint and several appointment.
- The difference between an appointed attorney and a replacement attorney.
- The powers they are giving to their attorney(s) and the range of decisions the attorney(s) can make.
- Whether there are decisions which they would not want their attorneys to make.
- That the attorney(s) can act even if the donor has capacity (unless there is a restriction in place in the LPA instrument).[37]
- That the LPA instrument can only be used after it has been registered with the Office of the Public Guardian.

---

[36] There are 2 types of LPAs – a Property and Affairs LPA and a Health and Welfare LPA. The 2 LPAs give different powers and authority to the attorney(s). The focus of this book is on Property and Affairs LPA instruments.

[37] This is not the case for Health and Welfare LPAs – even after registration, attorney(s) can only use it when the donor has lost capacity.

- That the LPA instrument can be revoked by the donor at any point provided they still have the capacity to do so.

- Whether anyone has told them to make the LPA instrument.

- Whether they have any concerns about the LPA instrument or who they are appointing.

The validity of an LPA instrument can be challenged on factual and prescribed grounds.[38] The prescribed grounds include lack of capacity and fraud or undue pressure being used to induce the donor to make the LPA instrument. This is when the statement of a certificate provider becomes crucial in establishing the validity of the LPA instrument.

The case of **TA v The Public Guardian** [**2023**][39] highlights the duties of a certificate provider. This was an appeal further to a decision made by HHJ McCabe in the Court of Protection in respect of the validity of LPA instruments which KA had made in 2021 appointing her daughter, TA, as her sole attorney to make decisions regarding property and affairs as well as her health and welfare. The Office of the Public Guardian challenged the validity of the LPA instruments on the grounds that the certificate provider had failed to make the requisite checks to verify KA's understanding of key matters. In the first instance, the attorney argued that the certificate provider was not required to carry out various checks of the donor's understanding – their role was to form an opinion of the donor's understanding. In this case, the certificate provider had simply asked KA whether she was happy about the LPA instruments to which KA confirmed she was.

HHJ McCabe did not agree with the attorney's position and held that this was not sufficient to simply verify that KA understood the scope of

[38] See Chapter 4 of this book for further grounds on which the validity of an LPA instrument can be challenged.

[39] TA v The Public Guardian [2023] EWCOP 63.

the authority she was giving and that she was not being pressured or induced. The Judge found that she was entitled to look for detailed evidence from the certificate provider. She held that the LPA instruments were invalid.

HHJ McCabe's decision was appealed. Mrs Justice Lieven considered the appeal and upheld HHJ McCabe's decision. She held that the Court of Protection was entitled to check how a certificate provider formed their opinion and this includes the steps they took before giving their opinion. The mere provision of a certificate in the right form cannot be sufficient on its own.[40]

> Author's note: This case is a reminder that the statement of a certificate provider is crucial. Certification is not a "box-ticking" exercise. Asking closed questions such as whether the donor was happy with making the LPA instrument is not sufficient. It is good practice for a certificate provider (whether they are a professional or lay person) to keep a detailed note of the conversation they had with the donor, such note to include the questions they asked and how the donor responded to them. The validity of an LPA instrument can be brought into question at a much later date and the certificate provider's recollection may not be as clear as when they first met with the donor. Keeping detailed contemporaneous notes which the certificate provider and the Court of Protection can refer to at a later date can prove to be material.

[40] TA v The Public Guardian [2023] EWCOP 63, para 30.

2.8 – The registration process

The making of an LPA instrument involves 2 stages: (i) the drawing up and execution of the form; and (ii) its formal registration with the Office of the Public Guardian. The LPA instrument has legal effect only after the completion of the second stage, that its, its registration.[41]

There is no longer a requirement for a donor to name people whom they would like to notify about the registration of an LPA instrument. This used to be a requirement in the older LPA forms where the donor had to either name at least one person to be notified about the registration and if no one was named, 2 certificate providers were required. From 1 July 2015, new LPA forms were implemented and the requirement to notify someone about the registration was removed.

However, a donor can still opt to notify people and list their names in section 6 of the LPA form. The people whom the donor chooses very often are those who they are closely connected to, and it is a way to make them feel involved from the outset, particular if they are not the named attorney(s) but are likely to offer support to the attorneys, when required. It could also remove potential suspicion in cases where a donor parent with several children appoints only a few of them and the remaining children feel they have been kept in the dark and may begin questioning the validity of the LPA instrument.

If the donor opts to notify someone, such notification is given to them by sending them form LP3. They then have 3 weeks to respond by completing form LP3 if they wish to raise an objection. Otherwise, they do not have to take any steps.

[41] To verify whether an LPA instrument has been registered, check the first page of the document. Upon registration, the Office of the Public Guardian will usually stamp the date of registration at the bottom of the page.

If there are no objections received, the Office of the Public Guardian will proceed with registering the LPA instrument. The registration attracts a fee of £92[42] per LPA instrument. The registration process can take 8-10 weeks[43] or even more depending on the backlog at the Office of the Public Guardian. The registration involves placing a mark at the bottom of page 1 of the LPA instrument stating the date it was registered. The original copy is then sent to the person who made the application.

Once the LPA instrument is on the Office of the Public Guardian's register, anyone can apply to obtain information on it.[44] A copy of the LPA instrument itself will not be released. Limited information will be provided which will include:

- The name of the donor.
- The name of the attorneys.
- The date when the LPA instrument was registered.
- The type of authority granted (that is, for property and affairs or health and welfare).
- How the attorney(s) are appointed, if more than one.
- Any restrictions placed on the LPA instrument.

---

42 This information is correct as of November 2025.

43 According to the OPG's annual report for 2024-2025, the average working days to register LPAs and EPAs was 49 days, https://assets.publishing.service.gov.uk/media/6878c0f77ea20916863638b1/opg-annual-report-2024-to-2025.pdf

44 This can be done by completing form OPG100 and there is no longer a fee payable to the Office of the Public Guardian to carry out a search of their register.

Author's note: There are undoubtedly benefits to streamlining the making of an LPA instrument and making it more accessible to those planning for their future. After all, LPAs are recognised as being an essential tool. However, what runs alongside the recent changes is the risk that by removing certain key safeguards, such as notifying at least one person about the registration, and placing increased pressure on the Office of the Public Guardian to process more applications within a reasonable period of time, there is likely to be an increase in invalidity claims.

CHAPTER THREE

APPLYING FOR A DEPUTYSHIP ORDER

The UK's population is ageing. There is a rise in our elderly population and a corresponding rise in people being diagnosed with progressive medical conditions such a dementia or Alzheimer's, which has an impact on their ability to make decisions for themselves.

There has been a strong push for people to put their affairs in order whilst they still have capacity to do so and are able to make choices. Creating an LPA instrument is one of them. However, there are many who have not chosen someone to manage their affairs. If their estate comprises substantial assets,[45] consideration should be given to the appointment of a deputy to manage their property and affairs.

There is a notable overlap between the previous chapter and this chapter since both, attorneys and deputies, have similar responsibilities and owe a fiduciary duty to P. The author will therefore keep this chapter on making an application to the Court of Protection for a deputyship order brief.

---

[45] If P's estate comprises receipt of state benefits, an "appointee" is usually appointed by the DWP to manage P's finances. The process to become an appointee is much quicker and their powers are limited.

Author's note: Deputyship orders made by the Court of Protection in respect of property and affairs are more common than deputyship orders for health and welfare matters. Those involved in P's care already have wide powers under section 5 of the Mental Capacity Act 2005 to make health and welfare decisions on behalf of P. The Court of Protection is therefore not keen to appoint a deputy for health and welfare matters unless the case warrants such an appointment – such as there is a history of disagreements within the family which means that decisions are not likely to be made jointly; a series of decisions will need to be made on an ongoing basis and turning to the Court of Protection for each and every one of these decisions is not pragmatic; P is at risk of abuse, etc.

3.1 – Identifying a suitable deputy

Deputies are not chosen by P. They are appointed by the Court of Protection to make decisions on behalf of P. In many cases, P's close family members or friends choose to take on this role and make an application to the Court of Protection, seeking their appointment. However, before an application is made, it is important to identify the most suitable candidate to put forward for the Court of Protection's consideration. The following factors should be considered by the applicant when identifying a suitable prospective deputy:[46]

- The deputy must be aged over 18.
- The deputy is not bankrupt or subject to a debt relief order, in which case they are not likely to be appointed.

[46] This is not an exhaustive list, and other factors should be considered depending on the circumstances and the value of the donor's assets.

- It is advisable for the deputy to be reasonably financially astute and have experience in successfully managing their own affairs.

- Whether the proposed deputy is familiar with the way P has managed their finances in the past and what P's future plans are, including their testamentary wishes.

Traditionally, the Court of Protection has shown a preference for appointing a relative or a friend of P, rather than a stranger, to act as their deputy. The primary reason for this approach is that such individuals are likely to have known P prior to the loss of their capacity. They are therefore more likely to be familiar with P's wishes, feelings, and financial circumstances and can draw down on this knowledge when making decisions on behalf of P.

Whilst there is still a preference for P's family and friends to be appointed as deputy, there are instances when this may not be appropriate. In **Re BM [2014]**,[47] Senior Judge Lush listed a few examples when the Court of Protection would not consider the appointment of a particular family member or friend:[48]

a) The proposed deputy has physically, psychologically, financially or emotionally abused P.

b) There is a need to investigate dealings with P's assets prior to the matter being brought to the court's attention, and the proposed deputy's conduct is the subject of that investigation.

c) There is a real conflict of interest.

[47] Re BM [2014] EWCOP B20.

[48] Re BM [2014] EWCOP B20, para 48 of the judgment.

d) The proposed deputy has an unsatisfactory track record in managing his or her own financial affairs.

e) There is ongoing friction between various family members, which is likely to interfere with the proper administration of P's affairs.

In cases where P has been awarded a substantial sum of money as compensation following a personal injury or clinical negligence claim, the Court of Protection would prefer the appointment of an independent professional deputy.

<u>3.2 – Ensuring the proposed deputy understands their responsibilities</u>

The scope of a deputy's role will be set out in the Deputyship Order. They are also required to have regard to the relevant guidance in the Mental Capacity Act 2005, Code of Practice. In brief, a deputy for property and affairs will have similar responsibilities to a property and affairs attorney.[49] They include:

- Handling P's money by dealing with their tax affairs; paying their regular bills and outgoings and paying off or managing their debts.

- Managing P's bank and building society accounts as well as their investments.

- Managing P's assets and property and ensuring that the property is maintained and insured – the deputy may require the Court of Protection's approval to sell and purchase property on behalf of P in the future.

[49] See Mental Capacity Act 2005, the Code of Practice and Chapter 2.2 of this book.

- Ensuring that P receives the pension and state benefits which they are entitled to.

As part of the application process, deputies are required to complete form COP4, which is also known as the "Deputy's Declaration". This is a detailed form and in sections 2 and 3, the proposed deputy is required to disclose information on their personal and financial circumstances. This is a helpful exercise as it helps the proposed deputy ascertain whether they are suitable to act and whether they are likely to be appointed by the Court of Protection. In section 4, the proposed deputy is asked to give personal undertakings and reminded of the main duties and responsibilities they are signing up to. In the author's view, the sections in this form are more informative and helpful to deputies than section 11 of the LPA form is to attorneys.[50] Form COP4 brings to the proposed deputy's attention specific and key responsibilities such as keeping their finances separate from P's and not using their position for any personal benefit, etc.

Author's Note: In most deputyship applications, the applicant is the proposed deputy. If they instruct solicitors or a professional person to assist them with making the application, the proposed deputy is very likely to have received legal advice on the scope of their powers from the outset. This differs from most attorneys who usually receive little or no legal advice when signing the LPA form.

50 Section 11 of the LPA form does not set out in detail what the roles of the attorney are. It summarises and highlights a few general points such as the attorney must act in the donor's best interests and act according to the principles of the Mental Capacity Act 2005 and its Code of Practice.

3.3 – The application process

The application can be submitted online (if the applicant is a solicitor, professional, local authority or their representative) or on paper (if the applicant is a lay person). The application involves submitting the following forms:

- Form COP1 – in this form, the applicant should set out clearly that they are seeking the appointment of a deputy to manage P's property and affairs and how this appointment will benefit P. If the application is made on paper, the applicant should complete section 5.1(a) and (b) with details of P and at least 3 other people who have an interest in the application.

- Form COP1A – in this form, the applicant should set out P's financial details. This information will assist the Court of Protection with gauging the suitability of the proposed deputy and set the level of the security bond.

- Form COP 3 – this form is to be completed by a suitable professional confirming that P no longer has the capacity to make decisions regarding their property and affairs. The Court of Protection will only appoint a deputy in circumstances where P lacks the capacity to manage their finances.

- Form COP 4 – this is the Deputy's Declaration. It is an opportunity for the proposed deputy to set out their personal and financial information and assure the Court of Protect that they are suitable to act by giving undertakings.

- Form COP24 – a witness statement is not necessary in straightforward applications. However, if P's estate is complex and/or there is relevant information which should be brought to the Court of Protection's attention, this can be done through this form.

- Application fee of £421.00.[51]

Prior to submitting the application, the applicant is required to inform at least 3 people connected to P about their application. This is done by sending them a notice (using form COP15PADep) that an application will be made. Those informed should also be provided with form COP5 in the event they wish to object to the application or seek a different order. Similarly, P should be informed about the application by personally being notified and being handed over forms COP14PADep and COP5.

Completed forms COP5 should be returned to the applicant within 14 days of receipt. If they are not returned, the applicant can proceed with their application.

3.4 – Appointment of a deputy and purchase of a security bond

If there are no objections, the Court of Protection is likely to make a decision without listing the matter for a hearing and appoint the applicant as deputy to manage P's property and affairs. At the same time, the Court of Protection will consider and make an order for the deputy to purchase a security bond and set the level of security. The Deputyship Order will not be sealed until the Court of Protection receives confirmation that a security bond is in place.

The purpose of the security bond is to insure the assets of P and offers the guarantee to pay any financial losses suffered by P, up to a specific amount, as a result of the deputy's misconduct during the course of their management of P's financial affairs. Should this happen, an application can be made calling in the security bond and the insurance company will compensate P. It is then a matter for the insurance company as to whether they will pursue the deputy for their misconduct.

[51] This information is correct as of November 2025.

Author's note: The purchase of a security bond to protect P's assets is a requirement only applicable to deputies and is a cost borne by P's estate. Given the protection and assurance that it offers, its importance does not go unnoticed. Surprisingly, although attorneys have responsibilities much like deputies, and could also potentially cause losses to the donor's estate, they are not required to purchase a security bond.

The author has acted in cases where costly High Court actions had to be taken against an attorney to recover P's assets. Had there been a security bond in place, expensive High Court actions could have been avoided. The author is of the view that there should be a similar requirement for attorneys to purchase some form of security bond at the time of registration to offer more protection to the donor/P.

CHAPTER FOUR

WHAT TO DO IF THERE ARE CONCERNS REGARDING AN ATTORNEY BEFORE THE LPA INSTRUMENT IS REGISTERED?

In the recent cases reported in the news,[52] the attorneys started abusing their powers following their appointment in this position of trust. But what if before their appointment, there are already concerns and/or evidence that the person whom the donor has chosen to be their intended attorney may not be trustworthy?

As a reminder, an LPA instrument unregistered with the Office of the Public Guardian does not have any legal effect and cannot be used. Therefore, if one has concerns regarding an attorney who has been appointed by the donor, but the LPA instrument is yet to be registered, there is an opportunity to prevent them from being given powers by stopping the registration process. In this chapter, the author addresses the steps which can be taken to safeguard a vulnerable person before an LPA instrument is registered.

4.1 – Case Study: Abdel (Part 1)

Abdel and Sabah have 2 children – Mo and Jasmine. During the course of their marriage, they acquired two properties: their family home as well as a holiday home in Cumbria which they rent out. 15 years ago, Abdel and Sabah made a Lasting Power of Attorney. They decided to appoint each other as their attorney, with no provisions made for a

[52] See Chapter 1.2 of this book.

replacement attorney. They did not appoint their children. At the time, their children were under the age of 18 years.

Sabah died 2 years ago and left her estate to Abdel. It was agreed at the time that Jasmine would move in with Abdel to look after him during the week and Mo would visit at weekends to give Jasmine a break. It seemed like a sensible arrangement since Jasmine was not working at the time. It later transpired that Jasmine had been dismissed from her role as a credit controller.

Around a year ago, Mo noticed that Sabah's jewellery had gone missing. He also noticed that Abdel no longer wore his Rolex watch, a gift from Sabah which Abdel was attached to. When questioned about its whereabouts, Abdel said that he did not know where his watch was, but he did not want to upset Jasmine by asking her.

Abdel's physical and mental health started deteriorating. At times, he appeared confused and forgetful. On one of his visits, Mo saw a Land Registry form showing that the holiday home had been transferred into Jasmine's name 6 months ago. Mo asked Abdel about it. Abdel was not sure what was going on and asked Mo to speak to Jasmine. Mo asked Jasmine why this had been done and Jasmine explained it was done to make it easier for her to rent the holiday home and use the income to pay for Abdel's outgoings. Mo found this odd since most of Abdel's outgoings were paid by direct debit and his pension covered these expenses. Mo checked Abdel's bank statements and there was no evidence that any rental income was being paid into his account.

Mo and Jasmine discussed with Abdel that he should appoint attorneys to manage his finances.[53] However, Jasmine was adamant that everything was working fine, and Abdel should not have to deal with paperwork unnecessarily. Abdel's condition kept deteriorating and it

53 The LPA which Abdel had previously made appointing Sabah as his attorney ceased to have any legal effect following Sabah's death.

became clear after a few months that he was no longer able to make certain decisions.

Mo started visiting Abdel more often and on one occasion, he saw an LPA form in Abdel's kitchen which had been signed that week. Jasmine was appointed as the sole attorney. Mo asked Abdel why he did not mention the LPA document to him or appoint him alongside Jasmine. Abdel was confused. He did not know what was going on but recalled Jasmine's friend talking to him about some papers which had now been sent somewhere to be "finalised".

Mo has concerns about Jasmine's motives and the way in which the making of the LPA instrument has been handled. He seeks legal advice on whether he can object to the registration of the LPA instrument.

The first step which Mo or his legal advisor should take is carry out a check of the Office of the Public Guardian's register to establish whether the LPA has already been registered. If it has not been registered, consider whether Mo can object to the registration of the LPA instrument to stop Jasmine from formally gaining control of Abdel's property and affairs. The author addresses the next steps which Mo should take in Chapter 4.5.

Author's note: As mentioned above in Chapter 2.8, there is no longer a requirement for a donor to give notice to certain individuals before the LPA instrument is registered. As a result, close family members (such as Mo in the case study above) and friends may not be aware of the existence of the LPA instrument unless they are notified or they find out by some other means. If someone has concerns and wishes to find out whether a registered power of attorney instrument exists, they can make enquiries by completing and submitting form OPG100 to the Office of the Public Guardian. Limited information will be provided by the Office of the Public Guardian – such as the date of the registration; the names of the attorney(s); whether decisions relate to property and finances or health and welfare; whether there are restrictions on the attorney's powers, etc. There is currently no fee payable for this search.[54]

4.2 – Who can object to the registration of an LPA instrument?

Those who can object to the registration of an LPA are:

- The donor of the LPA instrument.
- The attorney.
- The "person to be told", listed at section 6 in the LPA instrument and who will have seen form LP3.
- Someone who has concerns regarding the validity of the LPA instrument and/or the conduct of the proposed attorney(s).

4.3 – The starting point: on what grounds will the registration of LPA instrument be challenged?

The burden of proof rests with the objector who wishes to object to the registration of an LPA instrument. It is important to establish, from the outset, the grounds on which the registration of the LPA instrument will be challenged. This is because there are different procedures and forms to complete depending on the reasons for the objection. The objector is required to submit different evidence to discharge their burden of proof.

There are 2 main grounds on which the registration of an LPA instrument can be challenged. They are:

1) The factual grounds; and

54 This information is correct as of November 2025.

2) The prescribed grounds.

4.4 – Objecting on factual grounds and the procedure involved

One can object on factual grounds and the evidence required is usually easily accessible or available to the objector. The factual grounds are:

- The donor or attorney(s) have died.
- The donor and attorney were married or had a civil partnership but have divorced or ended the civil partnership.
- The attorney does not have the mental capacity to be an attorney.
- The attorney has chosen to stop acting, that is, they have disclaimed their appointment.
- The donor or attorney(s) are bankrupt, interim bankrupt or subject to a Debt Relief Order. This applies to property and financial affairs attorneys only.

The objector has 3 weeks, from being told about the registration, to object. Depending on who the objector is, the following forms together with the relevant evidence should be completed and submitted to the Office of the Public Guardian:

Objection by the donor

Complete form LPA006 and explain the reasons for objecting to the registration. The Office of the Public Guardian will suspend the LPA instrument. The intended attorney(s) will not be able to use it unless they apply to the Court of Protection and a court order is made directing the Public Guardian to register the LPA instrument.

Objection by the attorney or the person who has been notified

Complete form LPA007 and provide the relevant evidence depending on the factual ground(s) – such as the death certificate, the attorney's mental capacity report, the disclaimer signed by the attorney, the bankruptcy order, etc.

> Author's note: At this stage, it is sufficient to inform the Office of the Public Guardian only. The Office of the Public Guardian will respond to the objector and inform them if they are going to stop the registration or not. The Court of Protection does not become involved unless the objection is on prescribed grounds.

4.5 – Objecting on prescribed grounds and the procedure involved

One can object to the registration of an LPA instrument on prescribed grounds. The evidence required is more complex and this may explain why the Court of Protection becomes involved when an objection is made on these grounds. Section 22(4)(a) of the Mental Capacity Act 2005 empowers the Court of Protection to "*direct that an instrument purporting to create the lasting power of attorney is not to be registered.*"

Since this matter involves property and affairs matters, the permission of the Court of Protection is not required before an application is made.

The prescribed grounds are:

- The objector does not believe the donor had the mental capacity to make the LPA.
- The donor cancelled their LPA instrument when they regained capacity.

- There was fraud, for example, someone faked the donor's signature.
- The donor was pressured to make the LPA instrument.
- The attorney is acting against the donor's best interests or proposes to behave in a way that would not be in the donor's best interests.

The objector has 3 weeks, from being told about the registration, to state their position to the Court of Protection and inform the Office of the Public Guardian. Depending on who the objector is, the following forms together with the relevant evidence should be submitted.

Objection by an intended attorney or a person who has been notified

Complete form COP7 and provide the relevant evidence to the Court of Protection. At this early stage, the objector may not have direct evidence of the donor's lack of capacity; fraud or undue influence exerted on the donor; or the intended attorney's conduct. In such circumstances, it is important to set out in detail the concerns which the objector has. This can be done by preparing a detailed witness statement (form COP24) and exhibiting relevant evidence which the objector may have in their possession.

Filing an application with the Court of Protection (by submitting form COP7) is only the first step. The objector must also notify the Office of the Public Guardian that they have made an application to the Court of Protection. This is done by completing and submitting form LPA008 to the Office of the Public Guardian within 3 weeks. Failure to do so may result in the LPA instrument being registered by the Office of the Public Guardian. Once the Office of the Public Guardian receives form LPA008, they will place the application on hold until the Court of Protection provides further directions.

Objection by someone who has concerns

If someone (who is not the intended attorney or a person to be notified) has found out about the impending registration and has concerns, they can object to the registration by completing form COP1. At section 4 of form COP1, they should set out that they are seeking an order for the LPA instrument not to be registered by the Office of the Public Guardian. The objector can provide evidence of their concerns by competing form COP24, if required.

There is an application fee payable by the objector at the time the application is filed.[55] It is important that the objector notifies the Office of the Public Guardian that they have made an application to the Court of Protection. This is done by completing and submitting form LPA008 to the Office of the Public Guardian within 3 weeks. Failure to do so may result in the LPA instrument being registered by the Office of the Public Guardian. Once the Office of the Public Guardian receives form LPA008, they will place the application on hold until the Court of Protection provides further directions.

After receipt of form COP1 (and form COP24, if further evidence is provided by the objector), the Court of Protection will inform the objector of the next steps which will include whether a hearing will be listed to address their objection and the directions to follow.

4.6 – Prescribed objections commonly raised

Objections on factual grounds are seldom contentious since the evidence speaks for itself and is rarely disputed. On the other hand, objections on prescribed grounds can become contentious as the evidence is not always straightforward.

---

[55] The application fee is £421.00. This information is correct as of November 2025.

An intended attorney has acted against the donor's best interests (or they intend to do so)

It is commonly cited by objectors that the intended attorney has behaved or will behave in a way which would contravene their authority and/or would not be in the donor's best interests. This may involve the objector proving a future intent of an intended attorney about something which is yet to happen, making it a difficult task. So, how should an objector deal with proving this?

Objectors are reminded that the Court of Protection will ultimately consider what is in the donor's best interests, if the donor lacks capacity. In doing so, they will assess whether the intended attorney can be trusted to act for the purposes for which they are being appointed. When setting out their evidence on an intended attorney's conduct, the objector should consider including the following, if applicable:

- Set out a pattern of destructive behaviour or actions taken by the intended attorney, such as:

    - The intended attorney's past behaviour or action: (i) give examples of actions taken by the intended attorney and explain how the action had a negative impact on the donor; (ii) whether the implications of the past action are serious enough to justify not respecting the donor's wishes; (iii) did the intended attorney rectify the matter and learn from their past action?

    - Was the intended attorney acting in a different capacity at the time? If so, what are the parallels with their role as an attorney? For instance, did they hold a position of trust or does the past action have no relevance to the management of the donor's finances?

- Future intent: If the intended attorney intends to act against the donor's best interests, (i) identify what the alleged behaviour is; (ii) how it is it likely to cause a loss to or harm the donor; (iii) if possible, set out a "before and after" scenario.

- Is there likely to be a conflict of interest between the intended attorney and the donor given their financial circumstances and connections?

- Is there conflict within the donor's family which will affect the intended attorney's judgment and management of the donor's finances? [56]

The LPA instrument is not valid because the donor did not have the mental capacity to make the LPA instrument

This is another commonly cited ground for objecting to the registration of an LPA instrument. There is a presumption of capacity under the Mental Capacity Act 2005, and the burden of proof is on the objector to displace this presumption. Capacity is "decision-specific" as well as "time-specific". In other words, the question which the objector should ask themselves is – "Did the donor have the capacity to make the LPA instrument when they gave instructions for and/or executed the document?"

As a reminder, a donor is deemed to have the capacity to make an LPA instrument if they understand certain relevant information including: (i) the purpose and effect of an LPA instrument; (ii) who the appointed

---

56 In the case of Re KC [2020] EWCOP 62, even though the capacity to make the LPA instrument was not an issue, given the difficult relationship of the 4 daughters/intended attorneys, the Judge applied the court's powers in section 16(6), the principles contained in section 1 as well as the best interests principles contained in section 4 of the of the Mental Capacity Act 2005 and did not register the LPA instrument. Instead, a panel deputy was appointed to manage P's property and affairs.

attorney(s) are; (iii) the scope of the attorney's powers including the scope of the assets which the attorneys can deal with under the LPA instrument; (iv) the LPA instrument can only be used by the attorney(s) after it has been registered with the Office of the Public Guardian; (v) the donor can revoke the LPA instrument at any time provided they have the capacity to do so; (vi) the consequences of not making an LPA instrument.

Very often, the objector is not in possession of a capacity report which is decision-specific as well as time-specific to support their position. In such circumstances, a detailed witness statement setting out their concerns regarding the donor's lack of capacity may be sufficient to satisfy the Court of Protection that around the time when the donor executed the LPA instrument, the donor did not understand or could not have understood the above information. The objector should consider putting forward the following evidence in support of their application, if applicable:

- Conversations with the donor when they showed signs of confusion – such as getting appointments and names mixed up, not understanding the full extent of their wealth.
- Occasions when the donor was forgetful – such as leaving the fridge open, misplacing items, not taking their medication.
- Lack of inhibition – such as walking out of their home in their night clothes or saying inappropriate things.
- Statements from neighbours, friends, carers, etc who had noted a change in the donor's behaviour or demeanour around the time the LPA instrument was made.
- Contemporaneous medical notes, if available.

After considering the above information, if the Court of Protection has reason to believe there are concerns regarding the donor's capacity to make the LPA instrument, it is likely to make an order which will include obtaining a capacity report and/or for the Office of the Public Guardian to make enquiries of the certificate provider,[57] before a final decision is made on the registration of the LPA instrument.

4.7 – Case Study: Abdel (Part 2)

In the case study mentioned in Chapter 4.1 of this book, Mo can raise an objection as someone who has concerns even though he was not notified of the impending registration of the LPA instrument. Mo is likely to object to the registration of the LPA instrument on a few prescribed grounds, namely: (i) he does not believe that his father had the mental capacity to make the LPA instrument; and (ii) Jasmine has behaved in a way which contravenes her authority or is not in their father's best interests.

The immediate steps which Mo should take are:

(i) As already mentioned in Chapter 4.1 above, carry out a check of the Office of the Public Guardian's register by completing form OPG100. If the LPA instrument has already been registered, Mo can consider making an application to have it revoked or cancelled. The author addresses this in Chapter 8 of this book. If the LPA instrument is yet to be registered, Mo can try and stop it from being registered

(ii) Complete form COP1, setting out what order he is seeking, that is, an order directing the Public Guardian not to register the LPA instrument.

(iii) Given that Mo is not likely to have a medical report to rebut the presumption of capacity or have supporting evidence on

57 The author deals with the importance of a certificate provider and keeping contemporaneous notes in Chapter 2.7 of this book.

Jasmine's conduct, he should complete form COP24 and provide detailed evidence to include:

- Why he believes that his father lacked the capacity to make the LPA instrument and transfer the holiday home to Jasmine. He can include statements from close family and friends who are willing to corroborate his concerns.

- How transferring the holiday home into Jasmine' sole name for no monetary value and without any satisfactory explanation has deprived their father of a substantial asset and is not in their father's best interests. Mo should be able to obtain some evidence from the Land Registry to support this.

- Highlighting a conflict of interest between Jasmine and their father since Jasmine may have put her interest first by keeping the rental income from the holiday home for her personal benefit.

- Concerns regarding Jasmine's motives and future intent. If Jasmine's employment as a credit controller was terminated due to the mismanagement of her employer's finances, Mo may argue that Jasmine is not suitable to manage their father's finances.

(iv) Submit form COP1 and COP24 to the Court of Protection and pay a court fee of £421.00.

(v) Complete and submit form LPA008 to the Office of the Public Guardian to ensure that they do not register the LPA instrument whilst the Court of Protection deals with his application.

4.8 – Objecting to the appointment of a proposed deputy

The author will keep this section brief given the overlap between objecting to the registration of an LPA instrument and objecting to the appointment of a proposed deputy.

To object to an application for the appointment of a deputy, the objector should complete sections 5.1 and 5.2 (if further information is to be included) of form COP15PADep. This form will have been served on them by the applicant before the deputyship application is submitted to the Court of Protection. The objector has 14 days to complete and return form COP15PADep to the applicant. The applicant will then submit their deputyship application together with completed form COP15PADep.

If someone is not notified of the application but finds out that a deputyship application has been submitted, they can object to the application by competing forms COP1 and COP24 and submitting it to the Court of Protection. Upon considering the application and objection (whether it is through form COP15PADep or the objector's forms COP1 and COP24), the Court of Protection will make directions which may involve listing the matter for a dispute resolution hearing.

Although most deputyship applications are uncontested, the ones which are contested arise mainly because of concerns regarding (i) the proposed deputy's suitability; (ii) concerns about the proposed deputy's past or intended conduct and trustworthiness; (iii) a potential conflict of interest between the proposed deputy and P; and (iv) conflicts or disagreements between the proposed deputy and P's close family and friends which may cloud the deputy's judgment when making decisions. In such cases, the objector should consider the points listed in Chapter 4.6 above and set out their concerns clearly.

CHAPTER FIVE

WHAT TO DO IF A REGISTERED ATTORNEY OR DEPUTY BREACHES THEIR DUTY?

An LPA instrument is often created as part of the donor's overall estate and wealth planning for the future, not necessarily because the donor is concerned that they are beginning to lack capacity. Consequently, in many cases where a Property and Affairs LPA instrument is made, attorneys do not start acting immediately following registration. The LPA instrument exists as a tool to be used in the future.[58]

It may therefore be years before an attorney starts making financial decisions on behalf of a donor. When they do start to make such decisions, there is a risk that the attorney may not find time to familiarise themselves with the Mental Capacity Act 2005, the relevant Code of Practice or seek any professional advice. They may start making decisions based on certain misconceptions;[59] or in some cases, the attorney may take advantage of their position after the donor has lost capacity and start acting in a manner which they know will cause harm or a financial loss to the donor.

In this chapter, the author addresses the key people and organisations to contact should the reader have concerns regarding an attorney's or a

58 The circumstances are different for a deputy who is appointed following evidence that P lacks the capacity to make certain decisions. Deputies therefore usually take on an active role from when the deputyship order is made.

59 See Chapter 1.2 of this book.

deputy's conduct, assuming that P is no longer able to engage and clarify issues.

5.1 – Contact the attorney or deputy

It may be helpful to address the concerns directly with the attorney or deputy. Very often, there is a simple explanation, and suspicions can be easily cleared with open communication. If the attorney or deputy took steps which resulted in them breaching their duty and causing a loss to P unintentionally, you can request that they rectify the position. In many cases, misconduct is unintentional, resulting from a lack of awareness or advice. An open conversation with the attorney or deputy may help resolve the issue and put P back in the position they were in before the action was taken.

It should be noted that if one raises concerns directly with the attorney or deputy, the attorney or deputy may not disclose personal or sensitive information relating to P, particularly if this is likely to put P at risk of exploitation. Attorneys and deputies owe a duty of confidentiality to P. A lack of response will therefore not necessarily indicate wrongdoing. However, in most cases where the concerns are unfounded, the attorney or deputy will engage and clarify any misunderstanding since it would ultimately be in P's best interests to do so.

> Author's note: Before making allegations of wrongdoing, consider whether P had the necessary capacity to authorise the attorney or deputy to take those actions. It is important not to adopt a blanket approach regarding P's capacity simply because they have been diagnosed with a medical condition.
>
> P may require some support from their attorney or deputy before making certain decisions independently. This is why it is essential for attorneys and deputies to record how and why decisions were made, such information to include: (i) the conversations they had with P; (ii) what led them to conclude that P retains capacity to make a specific

decision; (iii) any tools or support which was provided to P to assist them with making the decision; and (iv) P's reasoning behind the decision. These notes will prove to be useful in clarifying any misunderstanding.

5.2 – Contact the Office of the Public Guardian

Attorneys and deputies are accountable to the Public Guardian, and the Court of Protection when ordered to do so by the court. If you have raised concerns with the attorney or the deputy and they appear to be to be unnecessarily secretive and/or refuse to clarify simple matters which are not likely to harm P or breach P's confidentiality, raise your concerns with the Office of the Public Guardian. The role of the Public Guardian includes investigating concerns relating to registered attorneys and deputies and the Office of the Public Guardian has a separate investigations unit for this purpose.

It should be noted that the Office of the Public Guardian receives numerous referrals and will only investigate where there is a real concern regarding P. It is therefore advisable to put sufficient evidence before them to raise their suspicion. The author recognises that such evidence may not be easily available. In such circumstances, consider "joining forces" with others – such as P's doctor, carers, financial advisors, close family members – who may have similar concerns. If the Office of the Public Guardian receives concerns from independent and unrelated sources, they are more likely to carry out an investigation, as evidenced in the case of **Re DP [2014].**[60]

In this case, a social worker with the local NHS Foundation Trust first contacted the Office of the Public Guardian to express her concerns about the attorney's conduct after P had been found on a bus in a confused state. Since the concerns at the time related to P's health and

60 Re DP (Revocation of Lasting Power of Attorney) [2014] EWHC B4.

welfare and the attorney was appointed to manage P's finances only, the Public Guardian felt unable to intervene. Instead, the NHS Trust placed P under a safeguarding alert. The following year, a senior risk consultant with Aviva UK Life Financial Crime Team contacted the Office of the Public Guardian as he was concerned about the encashment of P's investment bond by the attorney. This led to the Office of the Public Guardian carrying out an investigation, which subsequently resulted in an application being made by the Public Guardian for the attorney's removal and for the appointment of a deputy to manage P's financial affairs.

Once you report your concerns to the Office of the Public Guardian, an investigations triage and support officer will look into them and decide whether further enquiries are required. If the concerns relate to the conduct of a deputy, the matter will be referred to the Supervision Team. If the concerns relate to the conduct of an attorney, the matter will be referred to the Investigation Team. Their investigations will include interviewing the attorney or the deputy as well as P in some circumstances; making enquiries of the certificate provider; sending a special visitor to assess P's capacity; reviewing financial documents; and preparing a report. If the Public Guardian [61] forms the view that there are valid concerns regarding an attorney's or a deputy's conduct, she may take several steps including:

- Asking the attorney or deputy to remedy the situation.
- Imposing close monitoring of the attorney or the deputy and expecting regular reports from them.

[61] The current Public Guardian is Ruth Duffin. This information is correct as of November 2025.

- Applying to the Court of Protection for an interim suspension of the power of attorney instrument or the deputyship order whilst further investigations are carried out.

- Applying to the Court of Protection to revoke the power of attorney instrument or the deputyship order.

- Applying for a deputy's security bond to be called in to restore P's estate if P has suffered a financial loss.

- Informing the police where a crime may have been committed.

To report a concern to the Office of the Public Guardian, it is advisable to complete form OPG130 since the information in this form will give the Office of the Public Guardian the necessary information they require to check whether they have the legal authority to investigate and there are credible concerns which warrant a formal investigation. The completed form can be posted to the Office of the Public Guardian, PO Box 16185, Birmingham, B2 2WH or emailed to them at opg.safeguardingunit@publicguardian.gov.uk. Alternatively, you can raise your concerns by telephoning them on 0300 456 0300.[62]

Once they conclude their investigations, the Office of the Public Guardian is unlikely to disclose their full report to the person who raised the concerns since the report will undoubtedly contain information confidential and personal to P. However, the Office of the Public Guardian may provide limited information and/or a summary of their findings and inform the person who raised the concerns whether further action will be taken by the Public Guardian. If there is a finding that P has capacity, the Public Guardian is not likely to take any remedial actions.

62 Information stands correct as of November 2025.

Author's Note: The Public Guardian's role includes investigating the actions of registered attorneys and deputies.[63] Due to the high volume of concerns reported to the Office of the Public Guardian and an existing backlog, it is taking several months for an investigation to get started.

In some cases where P is at immediate risk, waiting for the Office of the Public Guardian to conclude their investigations may not be in P's best interests. Other steps may need to be taken, such as making an application to the Court of Protection to seek interim orders.

5.3 – Contact the Bank

If the concerns relate to suspicious withdrawals of funds from P's bank account or transactions which do not follow P's known spending pattern, consider contacting P's bank. Banks will have their own policy on how to address financial abuse, and some have a customer care team or a team that specialises in supporting vulnerable customers.[64] The Financial Conduct Authority has issued guidance to banks and building societies on the fair treatment of vulnerable customers and many banks have also signed up to the 2021 Financial Abuse Code. Such guidance includes (i) understanding the needs of vulnerable customers; (ii) making sure their staff have the right skills and capability; (iii) responding to customer needs; and (iv) monitoring and assessing whether they are meeting and responding to the needs of customers.[65]

63 The Office of the Public Guardian's target time to investigate a reported concern is 70 days but it has taken them an average of 138 working days in 2024/2025 to deal with a reported concern.

64 From 7 October 2024, victims of authorised push payment fraud can seek a refund of up to £85,000 from their bank.

65 https://www.fca.org.uk/publications/finalised-guidance/guidance-firms-fair-treatment-vulnerable-customers

Banks have a duty to help victims of financial abuse regain control of their finances. Such help may include putting certain safeguards in place whilst their investigations are ongoing – such as restricting or removing any access which the abuser has to the victim's account or their bank cards; freeze the victim's account which will stop any payments or withdrawals being made whilst investigations are ongoing; give information to the victim on their assets, debts and their usual income and outgoings from the account to help the victim assess their current financial situation. If the bank feels that there is an immediate danger, they may alert the police.

Whilst, in theory, these safeguards can be put in place, in reality, where the concerns relate to the conduct of an attorney or deputy, it is very likely that the registered power of attorney instrument or the deputyship order has already been registered by the attorney or deputy with the bank, following which they were given access to P's bank accounts. As a result, there is a general reluctance for banks to investigate an attorney's or deputy's actions, particularly if the concerns are raised by someone other than the account holder or the attorney/deputy.

5.4 – Contact the Local Authority

Consider raising a safeguarding adult concern with the Local Authority responsible for the area where P is based, whether or not P is ordinarily a resident there.

Local Authorities have a duty to investigate matters where they suspect that an adult in their area is experiencing, or is at risk of, abuse or neglect.[66] This includes financial abuse comprising:

(a) having money or other property stolen,

(b) being defrauded,

66 Care Act 2014, section 42(1)(b).

(c) being put under pressure in relation to money or other property, and

(d) having money or other property misused.[67]

The Local Authority will make whatever enquiries it deems necessary and will decide whether any action should be taken to protect P's position, such action to include referring the matter to the Office of the Public Guardian and/or the police; or making an application to the Court of Protection.

5.5 – Contact the Police

The Fraud Act 2006 enables the police to take actions in serious cases of abuse and section 4 (1) of the Fraud Act 2006 states that:

"A person is in breach of this section if he –

(a) occupies a position in which he is expected to safeguard, or not to act against, the financial interests of another person,

(b) dishonestly abuses that position, and

(c) intends, by means of the abuse of that position –

(i) to make a gain for himself or another, or

(ii) to cause loss to another or to expose another to a risk of loss."

Attorneys and deputies hold a position of trust and if the concerns relate to their actions, consider referring the matter to the local police in addition to the other authorities mentioned above (such as the Office of the Public Guardian and/or the Local Authority). The police will get involved depending on the abuse which has taken place or is about to

67 Care Act 2014, section 42(3).

take place. As part of their investigation, they will interview the attorney or the deputy[68] (or anyone in a position of trust) and if there is evidence that the person concerned has misappropriated P's funds, they may take further action including prosecuting the person who holds a position of trust.[69]

However, besides the obstacles which the police often encounter during their investigations,[70] there are significant differences between a police investigation and an investigation conducted by the Office of the Public Guardian. This was highlighted by Senior Judge Lush in the case of **Re DP [2014]**:[71]

> *"When the police investigate an alleged crime, they need to consider whether there is sufficient evidence to present to the Crown Prosecution Service ('CPS') to guarantee a realistic prospect of conviction, which in this case would have been on a charge of theft or fraud by abuse of position. The CPS would have had to prove that JM was aware that he was acting dishonestly and they would have had to prove this 'beyond reasonable doubt', the standard of proof in criminal proceedings. The decision not to prosecute him simply means that the CPS was not totally confident that it would be able to prove JM's guilt so as to ensure a conviction. It does not imply that his behaviour has been impeccable."*

---

68 In the case of Re Buckley [2013], Nationwide had referred the matter to the police, and they interviewed and investigated the attorney in respect of the large withdrawals from P's bank account and the investment of those funds in a reptile business.

69 See Chapter 1.1 of this book – the author refers to cases where the attorney in question was prosecuted.

70 See chapter 1.1 of this book – the author's conversation with Paul Smith who worked for the police force.

71 Re DP [2014] EWCOP, para 44 of the judgement

The standard of proof in criminal cases is much higher, and this may explain why in some circumstances, the police will not take the matter further and suggest to the person raising the concerns that they seek legal advice since it is a "civil matter". It may be that the evidence which they have been presented with or which they have uncovered during their investigation is not sufficient to "prove beyond reasonable doubt" that the attorney or deputy has committed a crime.

The standard of proof in civil courts is "on the balance of probabilities". The evidential threshold is lower and the party advancing a civil claim is required to establish that the attorney or attorney has acted in breach of their fiduciary duty or in a way that is not in P's best interests.

5.6 – Make an application to the Court of Protection

As set out in chapters 5.2 and 5.4 above, where financial abuse has been identified by the Office of the Public Guardian or the Local Authority, they are likely to take the lead in making an application to the Court of Protection and bear the costs of making such an application until a costs order is made. The person who initially raised the concerns may become a party to the court proceedings and will therefore have the opportunity to set out their position during the course of the proceedings. However, due to the growing number of cases to investigate, the Office of the Public Guardian, the Local Authority and the police are not always able to conclude their investigations within a reasonable period of time.

Readers may find themselves in a situation where the investigations carried out by these authorities are taking too long and there is an immediate risk to P and/or ongoing financial abuse taking place which needs to be stopped. In such circumstances, if the person concerned has some evidence of the attorney's or deputy's misconduct, it may be appropriate to make an application to the Court of Protection to initially suspend the relevant power of attorney instrument or the deputyship order. However, in the author's view, this should be the last resort given the legal costs involved and the limited evidence an applicant may have at the outset of a case. It is advisable for applicants to seek legal advice before making such an application.

CHAPTER SIX

INSTANCES WHEN ATTORNEYS AND DEPUTIES HAVE BEEN REMOVED AND REPLACED BY THE COURT OF PROTECTION

The Court of Protection may revoke a Lasting Power of Attorney instrument under section 22(4) of the Mental Capacity Act 2005; and section 16(8) of the Mental capacity Act 2005 allows the Court of Protection to revoke a deputy's appointment.

There are several cases on the removal of attorneys and deputies following a finding that they breached their fiduciary duty and/or failed to act in P's best interests. Not all cases are reported. In this Chapter, the author refers to a few reported cases to give readers a flavour of the instances when the Court of Protection will not hesitate to cancel or revoke a power of attorney instrument or deputyship order.

6.1 – Ignorance is no excuse

Those familiar with the making of a Lasting Power of Attorney instrument will be aware that the process involves asking the attorneys to sign the form and confirm their understanding of their duty to act based on the principles of the Mental Capacity Act Code of Practice.[72] Similarly, when applying for a deputyship order, deputies sign form COP4 giving undertakings which include having regard to the Mental Capacity Act 2005 Code of Practice and acting within the scope of the

[72] See section 11 of a Lasting Power of Attorney instrument for further statements made by an attorney.

powers conferred on them.[73] However, in reality, when they eventually step up to their role, not many attorneys or deputies make time for reading and familiarising themselves with the Mental Capacity Act 2005, its Code of Practice, or to seek professional advice if they were in doubt. There is a tendency to rely on a few pre-conceived assumptions.[74] When questioned on their reasoning behind taking a particular action, very often, their response is that they thought they were acting appropriately. Examples of such responses are:

- *"[P] had capacity and said that I could have the money."*
- *"[P] would have wanted me to have the money if only they had capacity."*
- *"It will all be mine soon anyway, so what is the problem?"*
- *"I deserve this, for all the sacrifice I am making."*
- *"I will return the money, if [P] ever has a need for it."*
- *"If [P] does not mind and is well cared for, what is the harm?"*[75]

These are not reasons which the courts will entertain. There is a strong message which the Crown Court and the Court of Protection is sending – the courts will not sympathise with attorneys and deputies simply because they were unaware of the scope of their powers. Attorneys and deputies are expected to fully understand the extent of their authority and to act in accordance with the principles set out in the Mental

73 See section 4 of form COP4.

74 The author refers to the main misconceptions in Chapter 1.2 of this book.

75 This specific response was given by the attorney to the OPG's investigating officer. See the case of Re EG [2015] EWCOP 6, para 10.

Capacity Act 2005 and its Code of Practice. Failing to do so, even as a result of a lack of knowledge, does not absolve them of responsibility.

This was made particularly clear by Senior Judge Lush in the case of **Re Buckley** [2013][76], when he commented *"Ignorance is no excuse."* Case law shows that the Court of Protection is critical of such attorneys and deputies and will hold them accountable for their actions. In some cases, the Judge will even give permission to report the matter by naming the parties involved so that the public is made aware of what attorneys and deputies can and cannot do and what happens when they misbehave.[77]

6.2 – Main reasons for removing attorneys and deputies

There is little leniency shown to attorneys and deputies who have breached their fiduciary duty. The author lists below examples of actions taken or financial decisions made by attorneys and deputies which have led to their removal.

- Gifting of P's assets exceeding the limited scope of authority which attorneys and deputies are given.
- Loans made to the attorney or deputy or those connected to them.
- Any investment in the attorney's or deputy's own business.
- Unsuitable investment of P's funds.
- Sale of P's assets at an undervalue.
- Attorneys and deputies paying a "salary" to themselves.

[76] Re Buckley: The Public Guardian v C [2013] EWHC 2965 (COP).

[77] Re Joan Treadwell [2013] EWCH 2409 (COP) transcript, para 100.

- Transfer of P's funds or assets into the attorney's or the deputy's sole name.

- Occupation of P's property without making any contribution.

- Conflict between the attorney's or deputy's interests and P's interests.

- Failure to keep P's monies separate from their own.

- Using P's monies and assets for their own benefit.

- Failure to report and cooperate with the Office of the Public Guardian.

- Failure to cooperate with other professionals.

6.3 – Removal of Attorneys: Case law

Re Buckley [2013] EWHC 2695 (COP)

In this case, an application was made by the Public Guardian seeking an order for the Court of Protection to revoke the Lasting Power of Attorney in which Mrs Buckley (P) had appointed her niece to be her sole attorney. The LPA instrument was made on 7 September 2010 and was registered with the Office of the Public Guardian on 17 January 2011.

The application was not made by a concerned relative or friend of P. Concerns had been raised with the Office of the Public Guardian regarding the way the attorney was handling Mrs Buckley's finances which resulted in a formal investigation being carried out. The Office of the Public Guardian uncovered the following during their investigation:[78]

- Miss Buckley's house had been sold for £279,000 on 28 April 2011.

- Between 17 January 2011 and June 2012, the attorney had withdrawn £72,000 from Miss Buckley's funds to set up a reptile breeding business. The attorney claimed that this was a short-term investment which would generate a 20% return over a two-year period.

- The attorney admitted that she had used at least £7,650 of Miss Buckley's capital for her own personal benefit.

- The attorney said she visited Miss Buckley once a week, but this was contradicted by the nursing home, who said that she had not visited her at all until 16 October 2012, when she appears to have obtained Miss Buckley's signature on some unknown documentation.

- At one stage there had been daily cash withdrawals of £300 (the maximum amount) from Miss Buckley's Nationwide Building Society account.

- The Special Investigation Department at the Nationwide had alerted Social Services in April 2012 and the matter was also referred to the police, who interviewed the attorney in July 2012.

- Miss Buckley's estate may have incurred a total loss of approximately £150,000.

---

[78] Re Buckley [2013] EWHC 2695 (COP), para 10 of the judgment.

After gathering further evidence during the course of the court proceedings, the Office of the Public Guardian found that Miss Buckley had contributed a sum of at least £87,682.53 towards a reptile breeding business. What was particularly damaging is that (i) the business was registered in the attorney's name; (ii) the investment was not made in Miss Buckley's name; (iii) no steps were taken by the attorney secure Miss Buckley's investment – such as providing her with a formal guarantee or signing a declaration of trust to record Miss Buckley's beneficial interest in the business; (iv) the attorney did not seek advice from someone qualified on the investment; and (iv) the investment was a very high risk one and not compliant with the standard investment criteria.

The attorney's position was that she had made large withdrawals from Miss Buckley's bank account for her own use and to invest in the reptile business. Her reasoning behind her actions was that her aunt had given her money in the past and it was not an unusual arrangement since they were very close. Furthermore, her aunt loved animals and investing in the reptile business was what her aunt would have wanted.

Senior Judge concluded that the attorney was in breach of her fiduciary duty and had not acted in Miss Buckley's best interests for several reasons. These include the attorney investing Miss Buckley's funds in her own business; placing herself in a position of conflict; failing to keep Miss Buckley's money and property separate from hers; going beyond the limited authority to make gifts to herself. Accordingly, the LPA instrument was revoked, and the Public Guardian was directed to cancel its registration.

Re DP [2014] EWCOP 7

The Public Guardian made an application seeking an order from the Court of Protection that a Lasting Power of Attorney under which JM was appointed as a property and affairs attorney is revoked. In this case, concerns had previously been raised with the Office of the Public Guardian by a social worker regarding the attorney's conduct. However, this related to health and welfare matters and since JM had not been appointed as an attorney to make health and welfare decisions, the Office of the Public Guardian could not take matters further although JM remained on their radar.

The terrain changed when the Office of the Public Guardian received a tip off from Aviva in respect of the attorney's management of P's finances. JM had attempted to encash an investment bond in P's name and transfer the proceeds in his sole name. Since this was a property and affairs matter, the Office of the Public Guardian started a formal investigation which uncovered several irregularities in the way the attorney managed P's finances which included the following:

- JM paid himself a salary for the clearance of P's home and rubbish removal when attorneys can only recover out of pocket expenses.
- He leased a car under the Motability scheme available to P. However, this was not for P's benefit but for his wife's personal use.
- He gifted himself a sum of around £38,000 which was outside the scope of his powers under section 12(2) of the Mental Capacity Act 2025.

Senior Judge Lush considered the attorney's actions and concluded that the attorney had behaved in a way that had both contravened his authority and had not been in P's best interests. Accordingly, the LPA instrument was revoked, and the Public Guardian was directed to cancel its registration.

Re EG [2015] EWCOP 6

This is another case where the Public Guardian made an application seeking an order that the Lasting Power of Attorney instrument is revoked following their investigation. In this case, P had 4 children – one daughter and three sons. P had appointed her daughter and one of her sons as her attorneys for property and affairs. The daughter took an active role in the management of P's finances and gifted herself the sum of £15,000. She also gifted the sum of £20,000 to each of her three brothers, one of whom was her co-attorney. In total, the attorney had gifted the sum of £75,000 from P's modest estate resulting in P having only approximately £17,000 left in her estate. This was noted by the London Borough of Bromley, and they raised concerns with the Office of the Public Guardian.

The attorney who had made the gifts to herself and her siblings objected to the Public Guardian's application. Her position was that P had capacity at the time the gifts were made. P was aware that her daughter was in financial difficulties and had agreed to help her out. According to the attorney, it was also P's wish for her other children to be treated equally, hence gifts of £20,000 were made to the other 3 children.[79]

The Judge did not accept this and found that the attorney had signed cheques in her capacity as an attorney; the gifts far exceeded the limited authority given to the attorneys; and they had breached their fiduciary duty by taking advantage of their position. The Judge also found that even though her co-attorney had not signed the cheques, he was still a party to the transactions. The Lasting Power of Attorney instrument was revoked, and the Court appointed an officer from the London Borough of Bromley as P's deputy to manage her property and affairs.

6.4 – Removal of Deputies: Case law

Re GM [2013] EWHC 2966 (COP)

This case is different to the ones mentioned above in that the application was not made by a concerned party or the Public Guardian seeking the removal of the deputies. The original application was made by the deputies themselves seeking the Court of Protection's retrospective approval of a number of gifts which they had made from Mrs Meek's

[79] In this case, the attorney had gifted herself the sum of £15,000 instead of £20,000 since she had previously received the sum of £5,000 from P.

funds to themselves, their families, friends and several charities. Making the application had been recommended to the deputies by the Office of the Public Guardian following an investigation which uncovered these gifts. The applicants had no legal representation at the time they made their application, and the application lacked detail on the extent of the gifts which had been made by them since their appointment.

In this case, the Court of Protection had made a deputyship order on 25 August 2010 appointing MJ and JM (relatives of Mrs Meek) jointly and severally as Mrs Meek's deputies to manage her property and affairs. Following their appointment, the deputies started making several gifts and donations. Their reasoning behind these financial decisions, which they subsequently set out in their application, was "*We have acted as we thought the C.O.P. order granted us, enabling us to gift and donate in relation to the size of the estate. As GM is 92 years old we believe approx £200,000 to be adequate and if this is not enough [for her to live on], there is no way she will go short.*"[80]

Following the application, the Court of Protection made an order joining the Public Guardian as a party to the proceedings. Given that further information was required regarding the true extent of the gifting for which the applicants sought retrospective approval, the Public Guardian was ordered to prepare a section 49 report to address the following particular matters:

- Exactly how much had been gifted by the deputies, and to whom, and for what purpose.
- Exactly how much remained in GM's estate, including the assets that would have passed to her on Barbara's (GM's daughter) death in 2010.

80 Re GM [2013] EWHC 2966 (COP), para 13 of the judgment.

- The Public Guardian's view on whether it would be appropriate for the court retrospectively to approve any of the gifts made by the deputies and, if so, to what extent.

- The Public Guardian's recommendations regarding the future of the deputyship.[81]

During the course of the court proceedings, it transpired that the deputies were in fact seeking the approval of gifts of £231,259.50. These gifts included donations made to charities (£57,352.00); large gifts which the deputies made to themselves, and which included designer bags, watches and jewellery (£55,856.00 to MJ and £48,396.50 to JM); and large cash gifts made to various friends and family (£62,500). In addition, the deputies sought the court's approval of deputyship expenses in the sum of £46,552.24 in respect of a car and computer purchased by each deputy on the grounds that the car was used to visit Mrs Meek and the computer was used to keep an eye on Mrs Meek's investments online.

In his detailed judgment, Senior Judge Lush went through the legislation and Code of Practice applicable to attorneys as well as deputies when it comes to gifting on behalf of P. He recognised that to prevent the Court of Protection from being overwhelmed with applications, a proportionate and pragmatic approach would be to apply a de minimis exception in certain circumstances so that an attorney or deputy can gift a sum of up to £5,500.00 a year without the Court of Protection's approval – even if the gift does not fall within the limited scope of their authority as set out in section 12 of the Mental Capacity Act 2005.

The judge allowed gifts of only £73,352 (compared to the sum of £277,811.74 which had been gifted). This was broken down as follows: £57,352.00 to charities; £13,500.00 to those related to or connected with Mrs Meek; and £2,500 to a friend. As regards the remaining gifts, these were unauthorised and the judge found that the deputies had behaved in

[81] Re GM [2013] EWHC 2966 (COP), para 20 of the judgment.

a manner which contravened the authority conferred on them by the Court of Protection and was not in Mrs Meek's best interests. The judge had "no hesitation" in revoking the deputyship order.

Re P [2024] EWCOP 77

This is an ongoing case in respect of P's whereabouts as well as other health and welfare and property and affairs issues. For the purposes of this Chapter, the author will refer to the decision made by HHJ Burrows in respect of the deputyship order relating to P's property and affairs.

In this case, an application was made by the Official Solicitor for the removal of P's mother who had been appointed as his deputy for property and affairs in April 2020. P was a victim of an accident when he was a student at university. He had been struck by a vehicle whilst he was cycling and suffered a brain injury which left him with life-changing injuries and a disability. His quality of life will improve greatly if he receives compensation and it is understood that P issued a personal injury claim in February 2020 and a second set of proceedings were issued on his behalf by his mother acting as his litigation friend. The judge presiding over those proceedings had concerns about the way P's mother was handling the personal injury proceedings and invited the Official Solicitor to act as P's litigation friend in the personal injury claim. The Official Solicitor accepted and instructed Irwin Mitchell to act on P's behalf. Liability has been accepted by the defendant in the personal injury claim, and it is accepted that damages are likely to be in the millions.

To progress the personal injury case, the input of P's family and their cooperation is required, particularly on making contact with P so that a case manager can be appointed to provide P with support and therapies for his injuries. The solicitors representing P wrote to the mother (who is also P's deputy) on several occasions but did not have any response. As a result, the personal injury claim cannot progress, placing P's claim at risk.

At the hearing in respect of the mother's removal as a deputy, the judge asked the mother whether she would engage and cooperate with the solicitors representing P in the personal injury proceedings. Her answer was no. The Judge concluded that by not cooperating and engaging with the professionals in the personal injury claim, the deputy was not acting in P's best interests, and the deputyship order was revoked.

Re AECO [2025] EWCOP 5

This is an application made by the Public Guardian seeking an order to discharge P's deputy and revoke the deputyship order for property and affairs.

In this case, P's mother had been appointed as deputy on 24 June 2014. The Public Guardian raised concerns regarding her conduct. In the first instance, the Court of Protection suspended the deputy's appointment and appointed a panel deputy in the interim. At the hearing, HHJ Cronn addressed the following concerns which had been raised by the Public Guardian in their application:[82]

- Failing to report to the Office of the Public Guardian – the deputy accepted that she did not file annual reports on time and the most recent report did not contain all the documentation sought by the Public Guardian. Two reports were more than a year late and the last report was 7 months late.

- Failing to pay the supervision fee as it fell due – the deputy thought that she did not have to pay them as P was in receipt of benefits.

- Mixing money – despite being advised and reminded by letter by the Public Guardian and the general visitor sent by the Office of the Public Guardian, the deputy did not open a deputy's bank

82 Re AECO [2025] EWCOP 5, para 11 of the judgment.

account for P to keep P's funds separate. Instead, she received P's monies in her personal account and made payments on P's behalf from her account. The deputy admitted that she could not tell "whose money was whose".

- Occupying P's property – the deputy and her son moved in with P for extended periods of time and have not contributed to the additional costs of their occupation. At the hearing, she accepted that she owed P around £10,000 in this respect.

- Making concerning financial transactions including transfers to herself and her son – it appeared that large sums were paid to the deputy and her son which required further investigations.

- Not cooperating with professionals and the Public Guardian – the deputy had failed to file reports on time. In addition, she did not provide the Public Guardian with information requested relating to the investigation, nor did she provide any better information to the interim deputy.

Taking the above into consideration, HHJ Cronn found that the deputy had failed to perform her role, as a result of which P had suffered a financial loss. Accordingly, an order was made to remove the deputy and have her replaced by another deputy.

CHAPTER SEVEN

CHECKLIST FOR PRACTITIONERS – IS IT APPROPRIATE TO MAKE A REMOVAL APPLICATION?

As a reminder, under section 22(4) of the Mental Capacity Act 2005, the Court of Protection may revoke an LPA instrument if it is satisfied that (a) fraud or undue pressure was used to induce P to execute the LPA instrument or create the LPA instrument; or (b) the attorney has behaved, or is behaving in a way that contravenes his authority or is not in P's best interests or proposes to behave in a way that would contravene his authority or would not be in P's best interests. As regards deputies, under section 16(8) of the Mental Capacity Act 2005, the Court of Protection may revoke the appointment of a deputy if it is satisfied that the deputy (a) has behaved, or is behaving, in a way that contravenes the authority conferred on him by the court or is not in P's best interests; or (b) proposes to behave in a way that would contravene that authority or would not be in P's best interests.

The author has drawn down from her experience and put together a list of issues for practitioners to discuss with a client before an application is made to the Court of Protection. This list is not intended to be exhaustive. It serves as a guide when advising clients in the early stages of a case to help them make an informed decision. The checklist below will also help practitioners establish whether a proposed removal application is appropriate and likely to succeed.

7.1 – Who can take legal action?

If the donor has the capacity to revoke the Lasting Power of Attorney instrument, they can do so by a deed of revocation. In such circumstances, an application to the Court of Protection will not be required.

If the donor lacks the capacity to revoke their Lasting Power of Attorney instrument, before a removal application is made to the Court of Protection, invite the attorney(s) to disclaim. In cases where an attorney has misunderstood their powers and finds themselves out of their depth, this option may be a welcome relief. They can disclaim by completing form LPA005 and sending it to the donor, and any other attorneys named in the LPA instrument and the Office of the Public Guardian. In such circumstances, a removal application will not be required. A deputyship application to manage P's finances going forward would be more appropriate.

Otherwise, an application for the removal of an attorney or deputy can be made by other parties such as:

- A co-attorney or co-deputy who is concerned about the way the other attorney or deputy is behaving.

- The Public Guardian – the author has already referred to a few cases in Chapters 6.3 and 6.4 of this book where the Public Guardian took the lead and made a removal application after carrying out an investigation into the attorney's or deputy's conduct.

- A concerned party – such as a relative, friend or the Local Authority although it is recognised that legal costs can be a barrier for some public authorities.

In most cases, the client will be a concerned party, a co-attorney or a co-deputy. Such individuals can take legal action. Since the application relates to property and affairs matters, the Court of Protection's permission will not be required.

7.2 – The client's concerns

Whilst this may seem obvious, discuss with the client what their main concerns are. Is the client worried because they have been left out – for instance, one of the donor's children was not chosen by the donor to be an attorney and now thinks they are being kept in the dark? Or is there a genuine concern that P is being taken advantage of and is at risk of harm?

In this area of law, emotions run high and it is vital to manage the client's expectations from the outset. The Court of Protection is not a battleground for family disputes or power struggle. If you and the client are satisfied that the concern does not stem from the client's personal feelings but as a result of a genuine concern that P may be at risk, consider the next issue which is at the heart of any Court of Protection proceedings.

7.3 – P's capacity

It is important for the client to appreciate that the Court of Protection only has jurisdiction in cases where someone lacks capacity. There is a presumption of capacity under the Mental Capacity Act 2005, and one should be supported in making decisions by themselves. Even if they have been diagnosed with a medical condition or there is a registered power of attorney instrument or a deputyship order in place, consider whether that person retains the capacity to make the decision in question, if sufficiently supported. Before taking things further, it is important to explain the following to the client:

- The burden of proof rests on the client if they are to displace the presumption of capacity.

- A medical diagnosis of dementia or Alzheimer's does not necessarily mean that the person they are concerned about lacks capacity.

- Capacity is decision-specific as well as time-specific.
- There are different levels of capacity – it very much depends on the decision in question.

Once this backdrop has been set and the concern has been identified – for example, an attorney has made gifts to themselves or used P's funds for their personal benefit, consider the following:

- Did the donor have the capacity to make this decision? As mentioned above, there are different levels of capacity. The capacity threshold to authorise a small gift is lower than the capacity threshold to transfer a large asset.
- Is there a satisfactory explanation for the gift or transfer? For instance, were monies transferred for a specific purpose or was it a gift in line with the donor's gifting pattern?
- If the gift/transfer is substantial, did the donor seek and obtain independent legal advice?

The importance of having discussions on P's capacity is highlighted in the case of **Day v Royal College of Music [2013]**.[83] Although this case was not brought before the Court of Protection, it is relevant since it is a reminder to practitioners to explain the different levels of capacity to a client from the outset. Below is a brief summary of the case:

After P's death, his children challenged the validity of gifts made by P to his attorney from a joint account held in the names of P and his attorney. The monies in that account belonged to P and P had gifted small amounts over a period of time to make use of tax exemptions. The total amount of gifts being challenged was £36,000. It was the children's case

83 Day v Royal College of Music [2013] EWCA CIV 191.

that P lacked capacity when these gifts were made, and the attorney had breached his fiduciary duty. However, after considering the evidence before him, the trial judge found that P had retained sufficient capacity to consent to the making of these gifts – the gifts in question were relatively small, simple and straightforward.

> Author's Note: One of the key principles of the Mental Capacity Act 2005 is that someone is presumed to have capacity unless there is evidence to the contrary. Sadly, abusers often use this presumption as a shield when they are called to account for their actions. It is vital to regularly review a vulnerable person's capacity and seek the input of medical professionals when appropriate.

7.4 – Pre action communications

The author remains of the view that issuing court proceedings should be the last resort. It is advisable for the client, in the first instance, to engage in pre-action communications.

Communicating with the attorney or deputy

There may be a satisfactory explanation as to why an attorney or a deputy made certain financial decisions. It may be as a result of following the donor's instructions; after seeking professional advice; or the action was required and served the donor's or P's benefit.

It is advisable to put the client's concerns in writing and seek an explanation from the attorney or deputy as to their actions. At this early stage, it is important not to place blame, particularly in cases where there is limited supporting evidence. Adopting such a stance is likely to result in the attorney or deputy not responding or they may retaliate by making accusations against the client which in turn can lead to contentious litigation in the courts.

Communicating with other authorities

If there is no response from the attorney/deputy or their response does not alleviate the client's concerns, consider raising the concerns with certain organisations. Readers are referred to Chapter 5 of this book for further information.

In a case where the concerns relate to the conduct of a registered attorney or a deputy, the most appropriate authorities to refer the matter to are the Office of the Public Guardian, the Local Authority and the police. They have a legal responsibility and duty to investigate concerns relating to a vulnerable person.

However, investigations carried out by these authorities may take several weeks or months to conclude. There may be merit in raising the client's concerns with the above-mentioned authorities at the same time as the client raises their concerns directly with the attorney or deputy. If the attorney or deputy responds with a satisfactory explanation which alleviates the client's concerns, contact the relevant authorities and inform them that your client no longer has concerns. If your client is still concerned after receiving a response from the attorney or deputy, they will not have lost valuable time since their concerns have already been logged with the relevant authorities.

7.5 – Can the problem be rectified?

There are cases where an attorney or deputy took actions which are outside the scope of their authority because of a lack of awareness, not because they intended to harm P. The author has been involved in cases where, following the receipt of a letter setting out her client's concerns, an attorney sought their own legal advice and offered to rectify the issue by paying back some funds.

If an attorney or deputy takes these steps and P is put back in the position they were in before the action was taken, it may not be appropriate to make an application for their removal. Although ignorance is no excuse,[84] the fact that the attorney or deputy has acknowledged their wrongdoing and rectified the problem will be a factor which will be considered by the Court of Protection. A removal application involves departing from (i) the donor's known wishes at a time when they had the capacity to make a power of attorney instrument (in the case of attorneys); and (ii) a decision previously made by the Court of Protection (in the case of deputies). The Court of Protection is usually reluctant to remove an attorney or a deputy unless there is evidence that P remains at risk and it would not be in P's best interests for the attorney or deputy to continue making financial decisions on their behalf.

If the client remains concerned about an attorney's disregard for the law, as mentioned in Chapter 7.1 above, explore with the attorney(s) whether they are willing to disclaim.

Author's Note: Even after a wrongdoing is rectified, the client should keep open communications with the attorney or deputy and recommend they seek guidance from the Office of the Public Guardian before major financial decisions are made. If the attorney or deputy continues to act unlawfully and a subsequent removal application becomes necessary, there will be a record that they had been advised to seek guidance and failed to comply. In such circumstances, the Court of Protection is unlikely to find sympathy for an attorney or deputy who argues they were unaware of the scope of their powers.

7.6 – Is there sufficient evidence to make an application?

If pre-action communications have been unsuccessful and the client's instructions are to make a removal application, start collating key evidence to support the application. In the majority of removal cases, the

84 The author refers to Senior Judge Lush's judgment in the case of Re Buckley [2013] EWHC 2965 (COP).

concerns involve (i) the donor not having the capacity to make the power of attorney instrument; (ii) the donor or P not having the capacity to make certain financial decisions or authorise the attorney or deputy to make such decisions on their behalf; (iii) the attorney or deputy has behaved in a way that contravenes their authority or is not in P's best interests; (iv) the attorney or deputy proposes to behave in a way that would contravene their authority or would not be in P's best interests.

In such cases, discuss with the client what evidence they have in respect of (i) the donor's or P's capacity; and/or (ii) misconduct of the attorney or deputy. The evidence required for the purpose of making a removal application is similar to the evidence which an objector is required to put forward when objecting to the registration of a power of attorney instrument or the appointment of a deputy. This is addressed in Chapter 4.6 of this book, and the author repeats some of the points below.

Evidence of lack of capacity

The author has already mentioned that a capacity report may not be available to the client at this early stage. In such circumstances, consider putting together a witness statement dealing with the following key issues, if applicable:

- Conversations with the donor when they showed signs of confusion – such as getting appointments and names mixed up, not understanding the full extent of their wealth.

- Occasions when the donor was forgetful – such as leaving the fridge door open, misplacing items, not taking their medication.

- Lack of inhibition – such as walking out of their home in their night clothes or making inappropriate comments.

- Statements from neighbours, friends, carers, etc who have noted a change in the donor's behaviour or demeanour, and which brings into question their capacity to make the LPA instrument and certain financial decisions.

- Contemporaneous medical notes, if available.

This will assist the Court of Protection in deciding whether there is sufficient evidence to make a declaration under section 48 of the Mental capacity Act 2005 that P lacks capacity. The Court of Protection is then likely to make an order seeking a section 49 report or a detailed assessment of P's capacity[85] which will include P's capacity to (i) manage their financial affairs; (ii) direct the attorney to make decisions on their behalf; (iii) instruct the attorney to account for their actions under the power of attorney instrument; (iv) revoke the power of attorney instrument.

Evidence of the attorney's or deputy's misconduct

The client may not have sufficient evidence at this early stage, particularly if the concerns are in relation to funds being transferred from P's bank accounts and the relevant bank statements are not available. The position may be different if the concern is in relation to the transfer of P's property to the attorney or deputy for no monetary value. In such circumstances, supporting documents from the Land Registry may be available.

Where there is no direct or supporting evidence, consider putting forward the client's concerns in a comprehensive manner to raise the Court of Protection's suspicion. Include the following points in the client's witness statement, if applicable:

- Set out the concerns they have regarding the attorney's or deputy's conduct and how it is detrimental to P. In Chapter 1.3 of this book, the author lists a few telltale signs of financial abuse

85 This is particularly relevant to the donor of an LPA instrument or an Enduring Power of Attorney instrument which has not been registered with the Office of the Public Guardian.

such as – signatures on cheques that do not match; missing jewellery or other valuables; non-payment of P's care fees, regular outgoings or utility bills; controlling or restricting P's personal contact and communications with others; P looking dishevelled or malnourished.

- Set out a pattern of damaging actions taken by the attorney or deputy whilst acting in their formal capacity. Even if the attorney or deputy rectified their wrongdoing, their previous action is indicative of their disregard for the law.

- The attorney's or deputy's past wrongdoing, even if they acted in a different capacity at the time (such as an employee; an informal carer; a trusted relative; etc). Although it may not be directly relevant, it brings into question their motive and suitability.

- If the client is concerned about an action which is about to take place, (i) identify what the action is; (ii) how is it likely to cause harm to P; and (iii) if possible, set out a "before and after" scenario.

- Whether there is a conflict of interest, such the attorney or deputy living with P rent-free or without contributing to the additional costs.

- Whether there is conflict within the family which is affecting the attorney's or deputy's judgment and management of P's finances.

- Whether the attorney or deputy is not cooperating with other professionals.

- Statements from others who have similar concerns – such as friends, social worker, carers, neighbours, etc.

This will assist the Court of Protection in deciding whether there are concerns regarding the attorney's conduct and/or suitability which warrant an investigation. The Court of Protection is likely to make an order for the parties (in particular, the attorney or deputy) to disclose key evidence. In some circumstances, if the Office of the Public Guardian has already carried out an investigation or is in the midst of it, the Court of Protection may make an order to join the Public Guardian as a party to the proceedings and submit a detailed section 49 report which will address the actions taken by the attorney or deputy and whether they contravened their authority or failed to act in P's best interests.

7.7 – Is the application affordable?

Discuss with the client whether the proposed application is affordable. Applications of this nature can be costly. Some insurance companies have legal expenses insurance included within their main policy, and it is worth exploring with the client whether they or P are insured.

When it comes to applications relating to P's property and affairs, the general rule on costs is:

> *"Where proceedings concern P's property and affairs the general rule is that the costs of the proceedings, or that part of the proceedings what concerns P's property and affairs, shall be paid by P or charged to P's estate."*[86]

An application to remove an attorney or a deputy, particularly if contested, is likely to cost each party who is legally represented tens of thousands of pounds. P's estate is likely to bear the costs of the application, which will include not only the client's costs but also the costs of the other parties involved in the proceedings including the Official Solicitor's costs if they are appointed to represent P. It is

---

[86] Rule 19.2 of the Court of Protection Rules 2017.

therefore essential to carry out a cost benefit analysis with the client to determine whether the expected benefit will outweigh the legal costs and whether P's estate can afford to fund this application. If P's estate is not substantial or consists mainly of P's property in which P intends living for the foreseeable future, there is not likely to have sufficient cash to fund the application, and it may not be in P's best interests to make this application. The situation may be different if the attorney or deputy has misappropriated substantial assets from P and the long-term objective is to pursue them in the High Court to restore P's estate. In such circumstances, it is advisable to consider the prospects of such a claim succeeding in the High Court before a removal application is made. If the High Court action is successful, P's estate will increase in value and will be able to fund the removal application.

Author's note: The case of EG & Anor v AP & Ors [2023][87] is a reminder of the limited jurisdiction of the Court of Protection. The Court of Protection cannot determine third party rights. These disputes require a different forum. The extent of the Court of Protection's power is to authorise a person (such as the attorney or a deputy) to bring proceedings in a different court.

7.8 – Is there a replacement deputy?

The donor's capacity (as well as P's capacity) is paramount to any application made in the Court of Protection. If the removal application is successful, there will be a declaration made by the Court of Protection that the donor of the power of attorney instrument or P lacks the capacity to manage their property and affairs. Consideration should therefore be given as to who should then be appointed to manage their finances in the future. This should be discussed with the client in advance of preparing

[87] EG & Anor v AP & Ors [2023] EWCOP 15

a removal application and form COP4 should be completed by the proposed deputy at the time the removal application is made.

7.9 – Will further action be taken to recover P's assets?

Consider whether following the removal application, the newly appointed deputy will take further action to recover assets misappropriated by the attorney or deputy. This typically involves:

(i) Calling in the security bond if the case involves the misconduct of a deputy; or

(ii) Pursuing a High Court action against the attorney to recover misappropriated assets since attorneys are not required to purchase a security bond when they are appointed. If a High Court action is being contemplated, it is advisable to obtain a "fit to sue" report on the attorney to ensure that if the High Court action is successful, the attorney has sufficient assets to comply with the court order.

> Author's note: The main purpose of a security bond is to restore P's estate for any loss caused as a result of the deputy's wrongful act(s). Deputies should not assume that they will not be liable simply because they are insured. The insurance company may decide to take legal action against them personally to recover the sums they paid out. Alternatively, if the security bond does not provide sufficient cover, they may be pursued by P's newly appointed deputy. Deputies may therefore find themselves in a similar situation to attorneys – where they are personally pursued for the misappropriation of assets in the High Court.

CHAPTER EIGHT

PREPARING A REMOVAL APPLICATION

The author lists below the forms which an applicant or their legal representative will be required to complete to start a removal application. The forms are straightforward, and their purpose is to set out key and relevant information which will assist the Court of Protection with making a decision in P's best interests.

The key forms are:

- Form COP1 (Application Form).
- Form COP1A (Supporting information for property and financial affairs applications).
- Form COP1F (Supporting information relating to validity or operation of EPA or LPA).
- Form COP3 (Assessment of capacity).
- Form COP4 (Deputy's Declaration)
- Form COP24 (Witness Statement).

In the next sections, the author will provide guidance on what to include in the relevant forms and the common pitfalls to avoid when completing the forms.

8.1 – Form COP1

Form COP1 is the start to the court proceedings. This is a key document, and careful consideration must be given to the various sections within the form when completing it – in particular sections 1, 4 and 5.

Section 1

Section 1 helps applicants focus on the nature of the application and guides them as to the forms which need to be completed. For an application seeking the removal of a deputy, the applicant will be required to tick the following boxes under the "Deputy, proposed deputy or other" heading:

- Property and affairs (where deputy not required) – form COP1A.
- Other applications – form COP24.

For an application seeking the removal of an attorney, the applicant will be required to tick the following boxes under the "Enduring Powers of Attorney (EPA) or Lasting Powers of Attorney (LPA)":

- Question of validity or operation of an EPA/LPA – form COP1F
- Other applications – form COP24

There is an opportunity in section 1.3 to seek an urgent interim order or declaration. If the applicant is concerned that P is at immediate risk, consider seeking an urgent direction that (i) the deputyship order or power of attorney instrument is suspended and an interim deputy is appointed; and (ii) a special visitor is appointed to assess P's capacity, particularly if there are concerns that the donor lacked the capacity to make the power of attorney instrument or actions have been taken by the attorney or deputy on the basis that they have been instructed to do so by the donor or P. If professional evidence is required from third parties to support the applicant's concerns, consider seeking a disclosure order as well.

Section 4

In section 4, the applicant is only required to summarise the pertinent points of the application and what order they are seeking. It is important to make sure that it is drafted in a balanced manner. The applicant will have the opportunity to set out their position in detail in form COP24 (their witness statement).

For a removal application, consider seeking the following orders (in addition to the interim orders mentioned above):

- The attorney or deputy is removed, and the power of attorney instrument or deputyship order is cancelled by the Public Guardian.
- A new deputy is appointed to manage P's property and affairs.
- The newly appointed deputy is authorised to use P's funds to commence legal action against the former attorney or deputy to restore P's assets, if applicable.
- The applicant's costs to be charged to P's estate pursuant to rule 19.2 of the Court of Protection Rules 2017.

Section 5

Section 5 requires careful consideration, and the author recommends that the applicant refers to the relevant Practice Direction as well as the guidance notes in form COP1.[88] It is important to make sure that the relevant people are listed at tables 5.2A and 5.2B. Failure to include some

---

88 Practice Direction 9B of the Court of Protection Rules 2017 and the Guidance Notes on completing form COP1 Application Form, page 9-10.

of them (or failure to explain why they have not been included) is likely to result in delays and the applicant incurring substantial costs after the application is issued. For the purposes of a removal application, the respondent is likely to be the attorney or deputy whom the applicant is seeking to remove. Consider also adding the authorities who are aware of your concerns and have begun an investigation – such as the Office of the Public Guardian and/or the Local Authority. They may have key and relevant evidence to share with the Court of Protection and the parties to the proceedings.

As part of the application process, the applicant is also required to notify key people of the removal application.[89] The persons to be notified are likely to be P's close family members. The following list of people is ordered according to the presumed closeness in terms of their relationship to P. They should be notified in descending order (as appropriate to P's circumstances)[90] –

(a) spouse or civil partner

(b) person who is not a spouse or a civil partner, but who has been living with P as if they were

(c) parent or guardian

(d) child

(e) brother or sister

(f) grandparent or grandchild

(g) aunt or uncle

[89] Court of Protection Rules 2017, rule 9.10 and Practice Direction 9B.

[90] Court of Protection Rules 2017, Practice Direction 9B, para 7.

(h) niece or nephew

(i) step-parent, and

(j) half-brother or half-sister.[91]

In addition, other persons whom the applicant reasonably considers has an interest in the application may need to be notified – for instance, someone who provides P with care; a close friend of P who visits P regularly and is in close contact with the current attorney or deputy, etc.

Key points for applicants to note in respect of section 5:

- If P's child or sibling is to be notified, the applicant should ensure that all the children or siblings in that category are notified unless there is good reason not to do so.

- Do not limit notification to only family members based on their presumed closeness to P. In some instances, P may be closer to friends than family members and consider notifying them of the application.

- If an applicant chooses not to notify someone based on their presumed closeness to P,[92] a valid explanation should be provided in their witness evidence.

- The applicant should seek to identify at least three persons who are likely to have an interest in being notified that an application has been issued.

---

91 Guidance Notes on completing form COP1 Application Form, page 10.

92 Practice Direction 9B, paragraph 7.

- A person who has been named as a respondent in table 5.2A should not also be listed as a person to be notified in table 5.2B.

8.2 – Form COP1A

The purpose of this form is to furnish the Court of Protection with information on P's financial circumstances. This information is relevant given that the application relates to P's property and affairs and the way it has been managed by the attorney or deputy.

A co-attorney or co-deputy making the removal application is likely to have sufficient information to complete form COP1A. However, this may not be the case for a concerned party, particularly if the attorney or deputy has failed to engage with them. In such circumstances, the applicant should provide the Court of Protection with whatever information they have available to them by completing form COP1A. If it is not possible to complete this form, the applicant should explain this in their witness statement.

> Author's note: If an applicant does not have sufficient information on P's finances but is aware of those who hold this information, consider seeking an interim order for that particular person or organisation to disclose information before the application can progress. There is the option to seek an urgent interim order in section 1.3 of form COP1.

8.3 – Form COP1F

This form is only relevant to an application relating to an attorney acting pursuant to an Enduring Power of Attorney instrument or a Lasting Power of Attorney instrument. If the applicant is seeking to remove a deputy, they are not required to complete this form.

Form COP1F should be completed and submitted together with form COP1. It is a basic form, and its main purpose is to provide the Court of

Protection with specific details on the attorneys and the power of attorney instrument. The applicant is also required to state the order which they are seeking in section 2.5. As mentioned above, this should be kept brief – preferably in line with what they state in section 4 of form COP1. The applicant will have the opportunity to set out their position in detail in form COP24 (their witness statement).

8.4 – Form COP3

This is a vital part of the application. One of the fundamental principles of the Mental Capacity Act 2005 is the presumption of capacity, and the Court of Protection will only have jurisdiction if P lacks capacity. In a removal application, depending on the grounds for removal, it will be helpful to put before the Court of Protection evidence that P lacks the capacity to make certain decisions such as (i) making the power of attorney instrument; (ii) managing their financial affairs; (iii) directing the attorney or deputy to make decisions on their behalf; (iv) instructing the attorney to account for their actions under the power of attorney instrument; (v) revoking the power of attorney instrument.

If it is possible for a formal assessment to take place before the removal application is made, instruct an expert to complete form COP3[93] which will confirm whether, on the balance of probabilities, P lacks the required capacity to make the decisions mentioned above. The applicant should make sure that the appropriate expert is instructed. There is no requirement for a specific medical expert or professional to carry out an assessment. The assessor must, however, have the proper training and credentials and must also be an impartial and qualified person. The Mental Capacity Act 2005 Code of Practice lists several professionals who can carry out such an assessment.[94] Such professionals include P's GP or the consultant under whose care P is; an approved mental health professional; a social worker; a psychiatrist, a psychologist, a speech and

93 Form COP3 was updated in July 2023.

94 Mental Capacity Code of Conduct 2007, para 4.42.

language therapist or an occupational therapist. It is advisable to check the expert's credentials, qualifications and experience before deciding on whether they are the appropriate expert to assess P.

To assist the mental capacity assessor with preparing their report, it is advisable to prepare a detailed letter of instructions addressing the following:

- A reminder that the assessor must apply the five statutory principles of the Mental Capacity Act 2005[95] and the standard of proof required should be based on the balance of probabilities.
- An explanation as to why the application is being made to the Court of Protection.
- Provide background information on P's family dynamics and how the parties involved are connected to P.
- Inform the assessor of any other factor which may affect P's reasoning such as a recent bereavement or if P has been suffering from depression.
- Provide details of P's illness, diagnosis and prognosis.
- Provide details of P's assets, income and expenditure given that the application relates to the management of P's finances.
- Provide a copy of P's medical notes, if available and relevant.
- Suggest that the assessor talks to P about wider issues (based on the information provided as set out above) and ask open

95 Mental capacity Act 2005, section 1.

questions to assess the degree of P's understanding. Their questions should not be limited to "Yes" or "No" answers.

- Provide information on known communication tools and practical steps which should be used to assist P with participating in the assessment, such as using sign language or visiting P at a specific time when they are more likely to be alert.

8.5 – Form COP24

Form COP24 gives the applicant the opportunity to provide the Court of Protection with background information on P and explain why making the removal application is in P's best interests. It is important to put forward evidence which is relevant to the application in question. There may be a temptation for an applicant to vent their frustration in respect of past family disputes and pile on allegations which are not necessarily related to the application. Applicants should be advised that the Court of Protection will primarily be concerned with P's best interests and their jurisdiction does not extend to resolving family disputes.

The author has addressed the evidence which the applicant should consider putting before the Court of Protection in Chapter 7.6. Depending on the grounds on which the removal application is made – whether it is because the donor lacked the capacity to make the power of attorney instrument; or the donor or P lacked the capacity to authorise the attorney/deputy to make certain financial transactions; or the attorney/deputy has behaved in a way that contravenes their authority or is not in P's best interest; or the attorney/deputy proposes to behave in way that contravenes their authority or is not in P's best interests – consider including evidence in respect of P's capacity and the attorney/deputy's misconduct such as:

Evidence of capacity – in the event the applicant is unable to put forward a completed form COP3:

- Why the applicant has not been able to obtain an assessment of capacity report.

- What attempts (if any) the applicant has made to try and obtain a capacity report.

- Why the applicant knows or believes that P lacks capacity to make the relevant decision.[96] To this end, consider including the following in the witness statement:

  - Conversations with the donor when they showed signs of confusion – such as getting appointments and names mixed up, not understanding the full extent of their wealth.

  - Occasions when the donor was forgetful, such as leaving the fridge door open, misplacing items, not taking their medication.

  - Lack of inhibition, such as walking out of their home in their night clothes or making inappropriate comments.

  - Statements from neighbours, friends, carers, etc who have noted a change in the donor's behaviour or demeanour, and which brings into question their capacity to make the power of attorney instrument or certain financial decisions.

  - Contemporaneous medical notes, if available.

[96] Court of Protection Rules 2017, Practice Direction 9 A, para 14.

Evidence of misconduct

- Set out the concerns they have regarding the attorney's or deputy's conduct and how it is detrimental to P. In Chapter 1.3 of this book, the author lists a few telltale signs of financial abuse which can be included in a witness statement, if applicable:

    - Signatures on cheques that do not match.

    - Missing jewellery or other valuables.

    - Non-payment of P's care fees, regular outgoings or utility bills.

    - Controlling or restricting P's personal contact and communications with others.

    - P looking dishevelled or malnourished.

- Set out a pattern of damaging actions taken by the attorney or deputy whilst acting in their formal capacity. Even if the attorney or deputy rectified their wrongdoing, their previous action is indicative of their disregard for the law.

- The attorney's or deputy's past wrongdoing, even if they acted in a different capacity at the time (such as an employee; an informal carer; a trusted relative; etc). Although it may not be directly relevant, it brings into question their motive and suitability.

- If the client is concerned about an action which is about to take place, (i) identify what the action is; (ii) how is it likely to cause harm P; (iii) if possible, set out a "before and after" scenario.

- Whether there is a conflict of interest, such the attorney or deputy living with P rent-free or without contributing to the additional costs.

- Whether there is conflict within the family which is affecting the attorney's or deputy's judgment and management of P's finances.

- Whether the attorney or deputy is not cooperating with other professionals.

- Statements from others who have similar concerns – such as friends, social worker, carers, neighbours, etc.

The above relevant information should be set out in the form of a witness statement with documents attached as exhibits. Practitioners who have completed form COP24 in the past will be aware of its restrictive format which can make a long statement difficult to read and follow. In the author's experience, preparing a separate witness statement verified by a statement of truth and attaching it to a completed form COP24 is usually accepted by the Court of Protection. The statement of truth should be verified in the following terms:[97]

> "*I believe that the facts stated in this witness statement are true. I understand that proceedings for contempt of court may be brought against anyone who makes, or causes to be made, a false statement in a document verified by a statement of truth without an honest belief in its truth.*'

8.6 – Form COP4

If the application to remove the attorney or deputy is successful, P is very likely to need a new deputy to manage their property and affairs going forward. It is advisable to identify a suitable deputy to take on that role

---

97 Practice Direction 9A, para 10.

before the application is submitted. The author refers readers to Chapter 3 of this book which addresses the factors which one should consider.

In many cases, where the removal application has resulted in a breakdown in family relationships, it may be more appropriate for a professional panel deputy to be appointed.[98] The proposed deputy will be required to complete form COP4, and this form should be submitted together with the removal application.

> Author's note: If the applicant's long-term aim is to try and recover misappropriated assets from the former attorney or deputy, make sure that the following orders are sought when completing form COP1: (i) a deputy is appointed to replace the attorney/deputy who is being removed; and (ii) the newly appointed deputy is authorised to use P's funds to commence legal action against the attorney/deputy who has been removed.

98 A list of panel deputies can be found at https://www.gov.uk/guidance/panel-deputies-list-of-court-approved-professionals

CHAPTER NINE

ISSUING PROCEEDINGS AND GETTING TO THE FINAL STAGE

This chapter addresses the procedural aspect of making an application in the Court of Protection. The author recommends that the Court of the Protection Rules 2017 together with the relevant Practice Directions are referred to. Complying with the rules, practice directions as well as the directions ordered by the Court of Protection will ensure that the application is dealt with in a timely and cost-effective manner.

9.1 – Issuing proceedings and the application fee

Once the forms are completed[99] and the application is ready, submit a hard copy by post to the central office of the Court of Protection in London. Their details are as follows:

Address – Court of Protection, PO Box 70185, First Avenue House, 42-49 High Holborn, London, WC1A 9JA.

Email – courtofprotectionenquiries@justice.gov.uk

Enquiries – 0300 456 4600

There is a court application fee in the sum of £421.00[100] payable at the time the papers are submitted. On receipt of the papers, the Court of Protection will issue the application and allocate a case number to it –

---

[99] See Chapter 8 for the forms to be completed.

[100] Information stands correct as of November 2025 and it is advisable to check COP44 for the applicable fee before issuing the application.

this is normally stamped on the first page of form COP1. This is when the proceedings formally begin.

The Court of Protection will return a copy of the sealed application together with initial case management directions. Such directions usually include, but are not limited to:

- A declaration, under section 48 of the Mental Capacity Act 2005, that P lacks capacity and it is in P's best interest to make the order.
- The case management of the application and which pathway it is allocated to.
- Whether P should be joined as a party to the proceedings. In applications of this nature, P will almost always be added as a party. If there is no one suitable to represent P, the Court of Protection will invite the Official Solicitor to represent P in the proceedings.[101]
- Who should be joined as a party to the proceedings.
- Who should be notified of the application.
- Service and notification of the application.
- If appropriate, further evidence to be filed and served by relevant parties.

[101] Note: The Official can decline to act as P's litigation friend if there is no security for their costs or in cases where the value of P's estate is not substantial enough to justify the Official Solicitor's costs.

- Listing the matter for a 1st hearing or a case management hearing.

9.2 – Service and notification

It should not be assumed that the Court of Protection will serve a copy of the application on the relevant parties once it is issued. The Court will serve documents during the course of the proceedings but only in limited circumstances – such as serving an order or a judgment, an acknowledgment of service or a notice of hearing.

It is the responsibility of the applicant to serve a copy of the application on anyone named as a respondent in form COP1 as well as notify those listed. The Court of Protection will usually set a timeframe for the applicant to comply with service and notification, failing which Part 9 of the Court of Protection Rules 2017 will follow.

Serving papers on a respondent:

As a reminder, respondents are those who have an interest in the application or who are likely to be affected by the outcome of the proceedings. They will have the opportunity to be joined as a party if they wish to participate in the proceedings. Unless the Court of Protection sets other directions, it is the applicant's responsibility to serve the application on the respondents as soon as practicable and in any event within 14 days of the date on which the application form was issued.[102]

Key points to be aware of:

- The applicant should serve a copy of the full application which will include all the forms as well as the witness statement(s) and exhibits.

---

[102] Court of Protection Rules 2017, Part 9, para 9.6(1).

- In addition, the respondent should be sent form COP5 (Acknowledgment of Service/notification) for their completion together with the Guidance notes on completing form COP5.[103]

- The applicant should then complete a certificate of service (form COP20B) [104] and file it with the Court of Protection within 7 days beginning with the date on which the application was served.[105]

Notifying other persons of the application:

The applicant will be required to notify those listed in section 5.2B of form COP1 as soon as practicable and in any event within 14 days of the date on which the application form was issued.[106]

Key points to be aware of:

- An applicant is not required to serve a full copy of the application on those to be notified.

- Instead, the applicant should complete form COP15. This is a notice informing the recipient that an application involving P has been issued by the Court of Protection.

- Make sure to include the following information in the form: (i) the application involves P's property and affairs and (ii) what order(s) are being sought.[107]

---

103 These can be found on the gov.uk website.

104 Section 2.2 of form COP20B should be completed.

105 Court of Protection Rules 2017, Part 9, para 9.6(2).

106 Court of Protection Rules 2017, Part 9, para 9.10 (1).

107 Court of Protection Rules 2017, Part 9, para 9.10(1)(b)(c).

- In addition to form COP15, send a copy of form COP 5 together with the Guidance notes on completing form COP5.
- The applicant should then complete a certificate of service (form COP20B) [108] and file it with the Court within 7 days beginning with the date on which notification was given.[109]

Notifying P

If the Court has directed that P is to be joined as a party to the proceedings and the Official Solicitor has been invited (and agrees) to represent P in the proceedings, the applicant will be expected to serve a copy of the full application on the Official Solicitor [110] and directions to this effect will be made by the Court of Protection once the application is issued. The applicant will not be required to notify P in person in this instance.

In the absence of such specific directions, the applicant will be expected to notify P that an application involving them has been issued by the Court of Protection and applicants should be aware of the following key points:

- They are required to notify P in person and explain matters using means most appropriate to P's circumstances. If the applicant is not able to effect personal service, an agent should be instructed to notify P in their place.

---

108 Section 2.3 of form COP20B should be completed.

109 Court of Protection Rules 2017, Part 9, para 9.10 (3).

110 Readers are referred to paras 17-21 of the "Appointment of the Official Solicitor in property and affairs proceedings: practice note" for further information on how to serve a copy of the relevant papers on the Official Solicitor.

- A full copy of the application need not be served on P. Instead, the applicant will be required to complete form COP14 which should include the following information: (i) the application involves P's property and affairs; (ii) what order(s) are being sought; and (iii) how P will be affected if the application is approved by the Court of Protection.

- As mentioned above, form COP14 cannot simply be posted to P. It should be presented to P in person together with a copy of form COP 5 and the Guidance notes on completing form COP5.

- The applicant (or the person effecting service) should then complete a certificate of service (form COP20A) and file it with the Court within 7 days beginning with the date on which P was notified.[111] Form COP20A is more detailed than form COP20B and careful consideration should be given when completing it.

9.3 – Responding to the application

Those who are served or notified of proceedings will be expected to complete and file form COP5 to inform the Court of their views on the application. This must be done no more than 14 days after the application was served on them or notification of the application was given to them.[112] If they fail to respond, they will not have a say in the court proceedings and will be bound by any decision made by the Court of Protection.

The respondent or the person notified will normally provide the following information in the form:

[111] Court of Protection Rules 2017, Part 9, para 9.10(3).

[112] Court of Protection Rules 2017, Part 9, para 9.12(2).

- Whether they consent to the application.

- Whether they oppose the application or seek a different order. In such circumstances, they will be required to file a witness statement with evidence which they intend to rely on within 28 days of being served with the application.[113]

- Indicate whether they wish to be joined as a party to the proceedings.

A completed form COP5 will assist the Court of Protection with determining whether the case is to proceed to a hearing and if so, how to manage the case in the future.

If a person was not served with or notified of an application and they wish to become a party to the proceedings, they can do so by applying to the Court of Protection to be joined. This is done by completing form COP10. This form is straightforward, and the applicant is required to set out their connection to P and what their interest in the court proceedings is. They are also required to state whether they consent to the application; oppose it; or seek a different order.

9.4 – 1st Hearing / Case Management Hearing

Upon receipt of the completed forms COP5, the Court of Protection will serve a copy on the applicant and the other parties to the proceedings. If a party objects to the application or seeks a different order; or the Court of Protection forms the view that the matter should be listed for an attended hearing, the court is likely to allocate the case to the Property and Affairs pathway and set further directions as to the management of the case, which will typically include:

---

113 Court of Protection Rules 2017, Part 9, para 9.12(5).

- The interim suspension of the power of attorney instrument or deputyship order.
- The appointment of a panel deputy.
- Adding someone who has applied to be made a party to the current court proceedings.
- Directing that the case is transferred to the most appropriate regional court depending on where the parties are based.[114]
- Filing of further evidence which each party wishes to rely upon.
- Listing the matter for a dispute resolution hearing to determine whether the case can be resolved.[115]
- A direction for the parties to hold a round table meeting a few weeks prior to the next hearing.
- Thereafter, listing the matter for a directions hearing to determine certain preliminary issues and/or a final hearing.

It is not unusual in contested applications for there to be more than one hearing before a final decision is made. Hearings typically take place to

[114] Regional hubs are located at Leeds Combined Court Centre, Newcastle Combined Court Centre, Manchester Civil Justice Centre, Reading County and Family Court, Bristol Civil & Family Justice Centre, Cardiff Civil & Family Justice Centre, Birmingham Civil and Family Justice Centre.

[115] The Court of Protection will usually wait for a period of at least 3 months before listing the matter for a Dispute Resolution Hearing to allow the parties time to engage with one another and potentially narrow down the issues in dispute.

assist the parties and the Court of Protection to identify and focus on the central issues to the case; make interim declarations to ensure that P's interests are secured; deal with any applications made by one of the parties whilst the proceedings are ongoing; and set a timetable to a final hearing.

If counsel was not involved in the preparation of the application, now might be a good time to instruct counsel to represent the applicant or a party to the proceedings in court hearings. Readers are referred to the Court of Protection Rules 2017 for further information on how to prepare for a hearing and, in particular, how to prepare the hearing bundle and the preliminary documents.[116]

9.5 – Alternative Dispute Resolution ("ADR") / Round Table Meetings

The Court of Protection does not have the power to impose ADR on the parties. However, it is not unusual for the Court of Protection to list the matter for a dispute resolution hearing or direct the parties to attend a round table meeting or an advocates meeting in the first instance.

It is advisable for parties to engage in ADR to try and reach an early agreement. Communications between parties to avoid unnecessary litigation are very much encouraged by the Court of Protection. To narrow down the issues prior to a hearing, Judges are known to routinely include a standard direction in a court order requiring the parties to attend court an hour before a hearing to engage in discussions.

It is important to advise an applicant or a party to the proceedings of the importance of engaging in alternative dispute resolution and coming to a compromise. Parties may experience a false sense of security thinking that their costs will ultimately be borne by P's estate. However, this is not the case as the general rules on costs are not as black and white as one

[116] Court of Protection Rules 2017, Practice Direction 4B.

might think.[117] Parties should consider how the dispute can be resolved in a speedy and proportionate manner. In doing so, they should put aside their personal grievances against one another; focus on the facts before them; and consider whether P is at risk if the current attorney or deputy continues acting in their current capacity and a new deputy should be appointed to take over the management of P's property and affairs.

9.6 – 2nd Hearing

If an agreement is not reached and depending on the complexity of the case and the allegations made against the attorney or deputy, a second hearing may be listed to either further narrow down the issues or to deal with interim applications. The Judge may make the following orders to ensure that key and relevant evidence is before the Court of Protection, and the parties are ready for the final hearing:

- Permission for a party to file updated evidence and/or evidence in response to evidence filed by another party.
- If appropriate, direct the parties to hold another round table meeting or an advocates meeting following further disclosure.
- List the matter for a final hearing.

9.7 – Final hearing

A hearing fee in the sum of £259.00[118] is payable by the applicant. Depending on the number of allegations made against the attorney or deputy; whether there are conflicting reports on P's capacity to make the power of attorney instrument and/or make certain financial decisions; the volume of disclosed evidence and the number of witnesses expected

[117] The author addresses the costs consequences and potential risks in Chapter 10 of this book.

[118] Information stands correct as of November 2025.

to give oral evidence, a final hearing may be listed for several days. The judgment may be given at a later date should the Judge require further time to consider matters.

If the removal application is successful, the final order will typically address the following key issues:

- A declaration that P lacks capacity and it is in P's interests to make the order.

- The power of attorney instrument or deputyship order is revoked, and the Public Guardian is directed to cancel its registration.

- The interim deputy (if one was appointed on an interim basis whilst court proceedings were ongoing) is appointed as the deputy until further order.

- Costs of the application – which takes readers to the next chapter.

CHAPTER TEN

COSTS CONSEQUENCES IN THE COURT OF PROTECTION

Litigation can be costly and it is important for a party to understand how a Judge is likely to address the issue of costs at the conclusion of a case, whether the party is successful or not.

Some readers will be familiar with the phrase "*costs follow the event*" or "*the loser pays the winner's costs*" in general litigation. However, in the Court of Protection, different costs rules apply depending on the nature of the application – whether the application involves (i) P's property and affairs; or (ii) P's health and welfare. Each has a different costs implication which is set out in rule 19 of the Court of Protection Rules 2017. Since this book is on the removal of an attorney or deputy due to their mismanagement of P's finances, the author will focus on the costs rules relating to property and affairs applications. However, readers are referred to Part 19.3 and 19.4 of the Court of Protection Rules 2017 for further information on the rules relating to health and welfare applications.[119]

This chapter will address (i) the general rule on costs in property and affairs applications; (ii) when the Court of Protection may depart from the general rule on costs; (iii) cases where the Court of Protection has

[119] The general rule states that each party bears their own costs in proceedings involving P's personal welfare unless there are good reasons to depart from this.

departed from the general rule on costs; and (iv) what a party is likely to recover from P's estate.

10.1 – Property and affairs applications

The starting point is:

> "*Where proceedings concern P's property and affairs the general rule states that the costs of the proceedings, or that part of the proceedings that concerns P's property and affairs, shall be paid by P or charged to P's estate.*"[120]

In brief, any party who issues an application or defends such an application can seek an order that their costs are paid by P's estate. The costs mentioned in the above rule extend not only to the applicant's costs but also the costs of the other parties to the proceedings as well as the costs of the Official Solicitor or P's litigation friend if P is joined as a party to the proceedings. Legal costs (particularly in contested applications) can run into tens of thousands of pounds, and the total costs can amount to a staggering sum which P's estate will be expected to bear under the general rule. It is therefore of utmost importance that careful consideration is given as to whether pursuing an application or contesting an application is proportionate and/or is in P's best interests.

An applicant or the parties to the court proceedings may form the view that since P will ultimately be responsible for the payment of their costs, there is no financial consequence in fighting the case to a final hearing. This false illusion is recognised by the law. To deter parties from engaging in court proceedings without due care, the rules on costs in the Court of Protection go further and provide for instances when the Court of Protection may depart from the general rule.

[120] Court of Protection Rules 2017, Part 19, para 19.2.

10.2 – Departing from the general rule

Costs in Court of Protection proceedings remain at the discretion of the Judge and the Court has full power to depart from the general rule and determine by whom and to what extent legal costs are to be paid.[121] Although the Court of Protection does not make a habit of departing from the general rule (after all, the risk of an adverse costs order should not deter a party from bringing a dispute to the Court of Protection and to uphold what they feel is in P's best interests), there are instances when the Court of Protection will not hesitate to apply their discretion. In doing so, the Court of Protection will have regard to the following:

a. the conduct of the parties;

b. whether a party has succeeded on part of their case, even if not wholly successful; and

c. the role of any public body involved in the proceedings.[122]

The Court of Protection Rules 2017 go further and describe the conduct of the parties as being:

- *conduct before, as well as during, the proceedings;*
- *whether it was reasonable for a party to raise, pursue or contest a particular matter;*
- *the manner in which the party has made or responded to an application or a particular issue;*

---

[121] Mental Capacity Act 2005, section 55.

[122] Court of Protection Rules 2017, Part 19.5(1)

- *whether a party who has succeeded in that party's application or response to an application, in whole or in part, exaggerated any matter contained in the application or response; and*

- *any failure by a party to comply with a rule, practice direction or court order.*[123]

With litigation becoming more expensive, the author has noted that in some cases, the Court of Protection will take the lead and place parties on notice of costs from the very outset of a case by including the following paragraph in initial court directions:

> "*The parties are reminded that whilst the usual order for costs in property and affairs cases is that the parties' costs shall be paid by [P]'s funds, the court can depart from that position where, for example, a party has unreasonably pursued or contested a particular issue.*"

The conduct of the parties (before and during proceedings) is a key factor which the Court of Protection will consider when making a costs order at the conclusion of a matter, particularly where one of the parties asks the Judge to depart from the general rule on costs. Parties who are legally represented will receive advice on how to conduct court proceedings in a reasonable manner to avoid being penalised.

> Author's note: Departing from the general rule is not limited to an order that a party (such as the applicant or the objector) cannot recover their costs from P's estate, resulting in them bearing their own costs. The costs order can extend to the party paying not only their own costs but the costs of the other parties to the proceedings as well. This could be an amount in excess of one hundred thousand pounds depending on the number of parties involved. It is important that an applicant (or an objector) is advised of the potential risk of having a costs order made

[123] Court of Protection Rules 2017, Part 19.5(2)(a)-(e).

against them. Readers are referred to Chapter 7 of this book for what the client should consider from the outset, before a removal application is made in the Court of Protection.

10.3 – Reported cases on costs

The author has noted a change in the way the Court of Protection has addressed the issue of costs in recent years, particularly in excessively litigious cases involving the removal of an attorney or deputy. In the case of **Re PP [2017]**,[124] which involved the revocation of a Property and Affairs LPA instrument, District Judge Batten took into account several factors including (i) the conduct of the attorneys before and after the application was issued; (ii) the reasonableness of pursuing or contesting an issue; (iii) the manner in which the claim was conducted; and (iv) the prospects of success. The judge did not hesitate to find that the attorneys' conduct before and after the application was made (which involved using P's money to purchase a property after the application was issued) as well as their substantial and continued opposition to the revocation of the LPA instrument when there was considerable doubt that it would succeed, justified departing from the general rule on costs. In this case, the judge ordered that the attorneys should be responsible for their own costs in equal shares as well as pay for P's costs – P was represented by the Official Solicitor in this case.

A few years later, the author herself was successful in a removal application involving an attorney who had mismanaged her father's (P's) property and affairs and had failed to act in his best interests. The Court of Protection was asked to depart from the general rule on costs, and a costs order was made against the attorney. She was ordered to pay the applicant's legal costs and was personally responsible for her own legal costs. The main factors considered by the Court of Protection in this case when departing from the general rule were (i) the attorney's lack of

[124] Re PP [2017] EWCOP 29.

cooperation; (ii) her failure to engage constructively before and during court proceedings; and (iii) her failure to comply with the court orders.[125]

In the section below, the author refers to a couple of reported judgments where the applications involved P's capacity. These cases highlight the importance of recognising that the presumption of capacity remains a fundamental principle of the Mental Capacity Act 2005 and should not be casually dismissed or overlooked when making an application. These cases give readers a flavour of how the Court of Protection will apply its discretion as to costs in such instances.

In the case of **Re JBN [2019]**,[126] the Public Guardian had made an application, without notice, seeking the revocation of a Lasting Power of Attorney on the grounds that the attorney had not acted in P's best interests. The application was made following an investigation which raised concerns regarding the sale of P's property; the transfer of the majority of the sale proceeds (approximately £950,000) to the attorney; and the attorney mixing his finances with those of P. According to the Public Guardian, this placed P at risk of not being able to fund his future care costs.

In the first instance, the District Judge suspended the Lasting Power of Attorney instrument and appointed an interim deputy. The attorney contested the Public Guardian's application on the grounds that at the time the property was sold, and the sale proceeds were transferred to him, P had the capacity the make these decisions. The key issue in this case was whether P had the capacity to make decisions involving his property and affairs at that particular time.

The attorney was successful in getting the suspension of the Lasting Power of Attorney instrument lifted and reinstated as P's attorney. By the time the matter concluded, the attorney had incurred legal costs in the

---

[125] There is not a published judgment of this case.

[126] Re JBN [2019] EWCOP62.

sum of around £82,000 and he sought an order that his costs are paid by the Public Guardian, and not by P's estate pursuant to the general rule on costs. The Judge agreed to depart from the general rule based on the manner in which the Public Guardian initiated the application and handled it. In particular, the Judge noted that the Public Guardian:

- Had failed to give careful consideration to the evidence in respect of P's capacity before issuing proceedings. Had the Public Guardian done so, they would have concluded that the evidence was weak and insufficient to rebut the presumption of capacity.

- Could have avoided incurring substantial costs by inviting the attorney to instruct a joint expert to determine P's capacity or asked the Court of Protection to decide on the issue of capacity in the first instance.

- Sought orders of a very serious nature, such as the suspension of the Lasting Power of Attorney instrument and the appointment of an interim deputy, without notice to the attorney.

- Failed to recognise the attorney's cooperation to alleviate any concerns by offering to place funds in an account to cover all of P's care costs, thereby removing the risk of P not being able to fund his future care costs.

In a more recent case of **Andrew James Riddle v NA [2025]**,[127] the applicant, an experienced professional deputy was asked by the City of York Council to make an application to be appointed as NA's deputy for property and affairs. NA, in his 50s, had sustained frontal lobe damage as a result of an assault in 2003. The Council were concerned that NA could not manage his finances. He was in debt and there was a risk that he would escalate further into debt and ultimately lose all his assets. NA's social worker prepared a medical report (form COP 3) concluding that

127 Andrew James Riddle v NA [2025] EWCOP 39.

NA lacked the capacity to manage his finances. Based on this report, the applicant applied for a deputyship order on 6 October 2022. NA opposed this application and there were several hearings thereafter. In May 2024, the Court of Protection made an order seeking a section 49 report in respect of NA's capacity to make decisions regarding his property and affairs. NA represented himself throughout the application and was not legally represented.

A section 49 report was prepared by Dr Ormrod which concluded that at the time of his assessment, NA had the capacity to manage his finances. He also noted that "*…such a conclusion may be at odds with earlier assessments. However, in my opinion it is likely that there have been changes in NA's levels of functioning as a result of his decision to stop drinking and the support he has received in the last year.*"

The applicant accepted the findings of Dr Ormrod and on 13 September 2024, his application to be appointed as NA's deputy was dismissed. The applicant sought the payment of his costs pursuant to the general rule on costs. This was heard by District Judge MacCuish who held that there should be no order for costs on the basis that the application had failed; NA maintained that he had capacity before and throughout the court proceedings and was successful in showing this; the presumption of capacity had not been displaced despite the social worker's initial report in 2022; and NA had succeeded in objecting the application.

The applicant appealed this decision, and the appeal was opposed by NA. Ms Justice Harris heard the appeal and held that District Judge MacCuish erred in law by failing to exercise his discretion in accordance with the structure provided by the rules – that is, the starting point is rule 19.2 and then identifying the grounds which justify departure from this rule by reference to the factors set out in rule 19.5.

Despite this finding, when reconsidering the costs decision, the Judge found justification for departing from the general rule on costs. In coming to this conclusion, the Judge considered several factors including (i) the conduct of the applicant and NA and found that their conduct was not a relevant consideration in this case; (ii) the applicant failing in his application and he would have been aware of a risk of his application failing given that NA had made it clear from the outset that he opposed the application; and (iii) ultimately, NA was successful in defending the application on the basis that he had capacity. The Court noted "…. *as a matter of natural justice, it may appear perverse that NA should pay the costs of Mr Riddle – who is a complete stranger to him – for an application he did not invite, always opposed, had no choice but to respond to, and ultimately was successful in defending. Unlike Mr Riddle, NA did not choose this litigation. He is not at fault in any way. This has to be a weighty consideration in determining the issue of costs.*"[128]

Reported judgments over the last decade indicate an increase in the number of cases where the Court of Protection has considered or been asked by one of the parties to depart from the general rule on costs. From experience, the Court of Protection does not look favourably on a party who has wasted its resources and time (as well as the other parties' time) by not following court directions at all or in a timely manner. In such circumstances, the Court of Protection is likely to make a costs order against that party or no order on costs.

The following factors would normally play a role in departing from the general rule on costs:

- Whether there were good reasons to start the proceedings.
- Whether proceedings were launched into disproportionately.
- Refusal to cooperate prior to the issue of proceedings.
- The reasonableness of a party pursuing an objection which has poor prospects of succeeding.

[128] Andrew James Riddle v NA [2025] EWCOP 39, para 37.

- The motive of a party: does it originate from personal grievance or out of a genuine concern for P?
- A party's disregard for any directions set by the Court of Protection which resulted to further and/or unnecessary costs being incurred.
- Unreasonable refusal to engage in alternative dispute resolution.
- Whether P's estate can afford the legal costs.

> Author's note: Rule 19.2 of the Court if Protection Rules 2017 is crucial and serves a public interest by giving applicants some assurance that they will not be penalised for bringing concerns regarding a protected person to the Court of Protection's attention. One of the questions raised following the costs decision in the case of Andrew Riddle v NA [2025] and which remains the subject of debate is – will applicants be deterred from bringing applications, leaving people who need protection at risk?[129]
>
> Whilst the impact of this decision will become clearer in the next few months, the author recognises that litigation is not straightforward. Applications made in the Court of Protection, particularly if contested, will inadvertently carry an element of risk. It is incorrect to assume that costs will automatically be paid from P's estate in all property and affairs applications, regardless of the outcome. The case of Andrew Riddle v NA [2025] is a reminder that even if the application is made in good faith and the parties conduct themselves appropriately, costs orders remain at the court's discretion.

[129] This is correct as of November 2025.

10.4 – Recovery of costs

The Court of Protection will normally deal with the issue of costs at the conclusion of a case. A party who sought an order in their application that their costs is paid by P's estate should be advised that even if they are successful in securing such an order, their costs are likely to be assessed on a standard basis in the first instance. It is not unusual for a Judge to make the following costs order:

"*The costs of the [parties] shall be subject to detailed assessment on the standard basis and the certified amounts of the same will be paid from the funds of [P].*"

The implication of such an order is that the party will not necessarily recover all their costs from P's estate. They will recover the amount assessed by the Senior Courts Costs Office, unless an agreement is reached by the parties involved. It is therefore important to advise a client from the very start that even if the general rule provides for their costs to be paid by P's estate, they are not likely to recover 100% of their costs. They may end up being personally responsible for the shortfall, depending on the funding arrangement they have with their legal team.

There is a set procedure to follow when assessing costs and there are costs experts specialising in the recovery costs in Court of Protection matters. This procedure can take several months to conclude and involves incurring further costs. Once a Final Costs Certificate is issued, it is usually presented to P's attorney or deputy for property and affairs who will then reimburse the party for the costs they incurred in the court proceedings.

CHAPTER ELEVEN

MISCONDUCT DISCOVERED POST-DEATH AND CONCLUDING REMARKS

There has been a marked rise in the number of financial abuse cases making the news headlines. Does this increase reflect a recent trend of people taking advantage of a vulnerable person to boost their own wealth? Or has financial abuse always been a problem but previously went undetected because of a lack of awareness?

As a specialist dealing with contentious cases pre-death as well as post-death, the author has come across many cases of financial abuse committed by someone in a position of trust, which started prior to the deceased's death. Such exploitation usually becomes apparent when investigating the validity of a Will or a lifetime gift discovered post-death. Cases like these suggest that financial abuse is not a recent trend. It has been happening for a while. However, as a society, we are getting better at spotting the signs sooner and can help those being exploited during their lifetime.

Sadly, there are still many cases of financial abuse which are not detected at the time it is happening. What can be done if it is discovered post-death? Although the focus of this book is not on post-death litigation, in this concluding chapter, the author will summarise the main points which a personal representative and/or a residuary beneficiary of an estate should consider.

11.1 – Misconduct discovered post-death – Case Study: Sandra

Contentious probate lawyers will relate to the following case study.

Alan and Sandra had 3 children – Lydia, Crystal and Joseph. Alan and Sandra made their testamentary wishes clear from the very start. They treated their children equally and it was known within the family that upon the death of the surviving parent, whatever is left would go to the children in equal shares. Wills were made by Alan and Sandra to reflect these testamentary wishes.

Alan passed away first. He was a scientist and left behind an estate valued at £450k which included an investment portfolio totalling £200k and his half share of the family home valued at £250k. Sandra worked as a scientist as well. She had cash assets of £100k in her savings account and owned the other half share of the family home (£250k). Sandra inherited Alan's estate following his death. By the time Alan's estate was finalised, she had assets valued at £800k.

Soon after Alan's death, Sandra's health started failing. Sandra wished to put her affairs in order and discussed this with her children. They all agreed that Lydia should be appointed as Sandra's attorney to manage her property and affairs. At the time, Crystal and Joseph lived far from Sandra whilst Lydia lived only 15 miles away. Lydia had also reduced her working hours as an accountant to spend time with Sandra. There was not a lot to manage since Sandra remained living in the family home and her pension covered her outgoings. If anything, she often had a surplus which she transferred into her savings account, in the event she had to move to a care home in the future.

Sandra's health deteriorated drastically. She became incapable of managing her affairs and died the following year whilst still living in the family home. Lydia, Crystal and Joseph got together at the family home after the funeral and went through Sandra's Will. They were not surprised to find that Sandra had appointed Joseph as her executor and left her estate to the 3 children in equal shares. Joseph asked Lydia to provide him with their mother's papers. Lydia initially offered to handle the administration of the estate herself on the basis that she knew more about their mother's finances. When Joseph insisted on acting as an executor, Lydia became defensive. She complained how hard it was for her to look after Sandra on her own. She stormed out of her house and refused to answer Joseph's or Crystal's calls.

Joseph eventually got hold of Sandra's papers and noted that over a period of 6 months, at a time when Sandra lacked capacity, Lydia had used her position as an attorney and withdrawn a sum in excess of £100k from Sandra's savings account and transferred the investment plan which Sandra had inherited from Alan into her own name. Sandra's estate now comprised the family home valued at around £500k.

The above case is a typical example of financial abuse being detected post-death. Up until Sandra's death, Joseph and Crystal trusted Lydia to act in their mother's best interests. In the last year of her life, Sandra was forgetful and confused and became a protected person (P). However, her living and financial arrangements did not change much. She remained living at home and her outgoings were being paid by direct debit, as before. Joseph and Crystal therefore had no reason to question Lydia's actions after she took over the management of Sandra's finances in her capacity as an attorney.

What steps can Joseph and Crystal take after uncovering what Lydia did to benefit herself during their mother's lifetime? At the time, Lydia was acting in her capacity as an attorney and owed fiduciary duties to Sandra. In the next sections, the author explains why the Office of the Public Guardian and the Court of Protection will no longer get involved and what other routes are open to Joseph and Crystal.

11.2 – Who can help?

The dynamics change upon P's death. Seeking the help of the Office of the Public Guardian because an attorney or a deputy has abused their position is no longer an option. As a reminder, the Office of the Public Guardian have a team set up to investigate the actions of a registered attorney or deputy.[130] However, upon the death of P, the registered power of attorney instrument or deputyship order automatically ceases to have effect. In such circumstances, even if the abuse involves the actions of an attorney or a deputy which is detected post-death, the Office of the Public Guardian will not carry out an investigation.

As regards which jurisdiction applies post-death, making an application in the Court of Protection or pursuing an ongoing action in the Court of Protection is not an option. The Court of Protection makes decisions which are in P's best interests to protect them during their lifetime. Once P dies, the Court of Protection's jurisdiction comes to an end. If a case is to be pursued post-death, the High Court will determine these disputes.

> Author's note: If there were ongoing court proceedings in the Court of Protection during P's lifetime and P dies before the proceedings are concluded, the case will come to an end. A final order will be made reflecting this. If the Court of Protection fails to deal with the issue of costs, consider making an application using form COP9 to address this.

11.3 – Who can pursue a claim post-death?

In Chapter 7.1, the author lists the parties who can make an application to the Court of Protection in their own name where they have concerns regarding the conduct of an attorney or a deputy. If the applicant is successful with their application to have the attorney or deputy removed,

---

130 See Chapter 5.2 of this book.

very often, a new deputy is appointed to manage P's property and affairs, and permission is given to them to pursue the former attorney or deputy in the High Court to recover misappropriated assets.

However, as mentioned above, a power of attorney instrument or a deputyship order ceases to have legal effect upon P's death. Upon P's death, the executor of their estate will usually apply for a Grant of Probate (if a valid Will was made by P) or an administrator will apply for a Grant of Letters of Administration (in the absence of a valid Will). They are the ones with the legal authority to take control of the deceased's estate and administer it. They are also the ones with the legal standing to pursue the former attorney or deputy on behalf of the estate to recover misappropriated assets. A concerned family member or friend will not have the legal standing to bring such a claim in their own name.

Personal representatives of an estate owe a fiduciary duty to the estate and the beneficiaries. They are expected to act in a neutral manner, failing which they are at risk of being personally responsible for legal costs. They must therefore carefully assess the misconduct which they uncover during their administration of the estate and question whether it is in the estate's interest to bring a claim to recover the misappropriated assets.

Very often, concerns are brought to their attention by the residuary beneficiaries of the estate who are likely to benefit from an increase in the inheritance they subsequently receive should the claim against the former attorney or deputy be successful. Since beneficiaries do not have the legal standing to bring a claim in their personal capacity, it will be a matter for the personal representative to pursue. To protect themselves from being personally liable for costs, the personal representative should consider seeking an indemnity from the residuary beneficiaries or applying for a Beddoe order. However, in many cases, the potential claim is against one of the residuary beneficiaries who was the former attorney or deputy (such as Lydia in the case study mentioned above in Chapter 11.1) and they are likely to refuse to give an indemnity and/or oppose the Beddoe application. There are also cases where the former attorney or deputy is now the executor, placing themselves in a position of conflict.

If a personal representative decides not to bring a claim on behalf of the estate, there are options which a residuary beneficiary can consider and they include:

- Requesting that the personal representative assigns their right to the residuary beneficiary to pursue a claim on behalf of the estate.
- Making a derivative claim on behalf of the estate, with the court's permission.[131]
- Seeking the replacement of the personal representative of the estate in the first instance (particularly if they are the attorney or deputy who misappropriated assets), following which the replacement personal representative can bring a claim on behalf of the estate, with the backing of the residuary beneficiaries.

11.4 – Author's concluding remarks

Attorneys and deputies are reminded of their primary duty – to always act in P's best interests. If they fail to do so, case law shows that attorneys and deputies will receive harsh penalties, whether they intentionally misused their powers or not.

To those who are thinking of taking on the responsibility to manage someone's finances, the author strongly recommends that they familiarise themselves with at least the Mental Capacity 2005 and its associated Code of Practice and if in doubt, seek legal advice before agreeing to become an attorney or a deputy.

To those who have already been appointed as an attorney or a deputy, the author's message is to be mindful of the following key messages when making decisions on behalf of P:

[131] See the Supreme Court case of Roberts v Gill [2010] UKSC 22.

1. Do not assume that P lacks capacity simply because they have been diagnosed with a medical condition.

2. A power of attorney instrument or a deputyship order does not give an attorney or a deputy unlimited power to make financial decisions on behalf of P.[132]

3. An attorney or deputy who is not acting in P's best interests is likely to be removed from their position and pursued in the High Court to return misappropriated assets.

4. There is no guarantee that a party involved in Court of Protection proceedings involving P's property and affairs will recover their costs from P's estate. Parties should act reasonably prior to and during the court proceedings.

Finally…

Remember Senior Judge's words in **Re Buckley [2013]**:

- "*Managing your own money is one thing. Managing someone else's money is an entirely different matter*"; and

- "*Ignorance is no excuse.*"

[132] For instance, an attorney or a deputy cannot make a Will on behalf of P. They will require the Court of Protection's approval for this.

MORE BOOKS BY LAW BRIEF PUBLISHING

A selection of our other titles available now:-

'A Practical Guide to Probation Breaches and Other Applications' by Mark Thomas
'A Practical Guide to Remarriage and Divorce' by Cordelia Williams & Claire Howard
'A Practical Guide to Privacy, Transparency, Reporting Restrictions and Closed Proceedings in the Court of Protection' by Laura Mannering
'Beaumont on Barristers – A Guide to Defending Disciplinary Proceedings (Second Edition)' by Marc Beaumont
'A Practical Guide to Payments for Environmental Services' by Ben Sharples
'A Practical Guide to the Law of Pregnancy and Maternity at Work' by Rebecca Thomas
'A Practical Guide to Redundancy – Second Edition' by Philip Hyland & Collette Moore
'A Practical Guide to International Issues for Scottish Family Lawyers' by Susie Mountain, Donna McKay, Ken MacDonald
'A Practical Guide to the Law on Deprivation of Liberty' by Ben Troke
'A Practical Guide to Rights over Airspace and Subsoil – Second Edition' by Daniel Gatty
'A Practical Guide to the Law in Relation to Inquests' by Ramya Nagesh
'A Practical Guide to the Construction and Rectification of Wills and Trust Instruments (Second Edition)' by Edward Hewitt
'A Practical Guide to Data Protection in Social Housing' by Clare Paterson
'A Practical Guide to Spousal Maintenance – Second Edition' by Liz Cowell
'A Practical Guide to International Parental Child Abduction Law (England and Wales)' by Dr Onyója Momoh
'A Practical Guide to Deprivation of British Citizenship' by Sean Ell
'A Practical Guide to Commercial Property Service Charges' by Rachel Garton
'A Practical Guide to Clinical Negligence – Third Edition' by Geoffrey Simpson-Scott (Geoff)
'A Practical Guide to the Rights of Grandparents in Children Proceedings – Second Edition' by Stuart Barlow

'The Electronic Communications Code: A Practical Guide – Second Edition' by Kerry Bretherton KC, James Castle, Mark Loveday

'A Practical Guide to the Independent School Standards – September 2023 Edition' by Sarah McKimm

'A Practical Guide to Estate Administration and Crypto Assets' by Richard Marshall

'A Practical Guide to Parental Alienation in Private and Public Law Children Cases' by Sam King QC & Frankie Shama

'Contested Heritage – Removing Art from Land and Historic Buildings' by Richard Harwood QC, Catherine Dobson, David Sawtell

'The Limits of Separate Legal Personality: When Those Running a Company Can Be Held Personally Liable for Losses Caused to Third Parties Outside of the Company' by Dr Mike Wilkinson

'A Practical Guide to Transgender Law' by Robin Moira White & Nicola Newbegin

'A Practical Guide to 'Stranded Spouses' in Family Law' by Mani Singh Basi

'A Practical Guide to Residential Freehold Conveyancing' by Lorraine Richardson

'A Practical Guide to Pensions on Divorce for Lawyers' by Bryan Scant

'A Practical Guide to Challenging Sham Marriage Allegations in Immigration Law' by Priya Solanki

'A Practical Guide to Digital Communications Evidence in Criminal Law' by Sam Willis

'A Practical Guide to Legal Rights in Scotland' by Sarah-Jane Macdonald

'A Practical Guide to New Build Conveyancing' by Paul Sams & Rebecca East

'A Practical Guide to Inherited Wealth on Divorce' by Hayley Trim

'A Practical Guide to Practice Direction 12J and Domestic Abuse in Private Law Children Proceedings' by Rebecca Cross & Malvika Jaganmohan

'A Practical Guide to Confiscation and Restraint' by Narita Bahra QC, John Carl Townsend, David Winch

'A Practical Guide to the Law of Forests in Scotland' by Philip Buchan

'A Practical Guide to Health and Medical Cases in Immigration Law' by Rebecca Chapman & Miranda Butler

'A Practical Guide to Bad Character Evidence for Criminal Practitioners by Aparna Rao

'A Practical Guide to Extradition Law post-Brexit' by Myles Grandison et al

'A Practical Guide to Hoarding and Mental Health for Housing Lawyers' by Rachel Coyle

'Stephens on Contractual Indemnities' by Richard Stephens

'A Practical Guide to the EU Succession Regulation' by Richard Frimston

'A Practical Guide to Solicitor and Client Costs – Second Edition' by Robin Dunne

'Constructive Dismissal – Practice Pointers and Principles' by Benjimin Burgher

'A Practical Guide to Religion and Belief Discrimination Claims in the Workplace' by Kashif Ali

'A Practical Guide to the Law of Medical Treatment Decisions' by Ben Troke

'Fundamental Dishonesty and QOCS in Personal Injury Proceedings: Law and Practice' by Jake Rowley

'A Practical Guide to the Law in Relation to School Exclusions' by Charlotte Hadfield & Alice de Coverley

'A Practical Guide to Divorce for the Silver Separators' by Karin Walker

'The Right to be Forgotten – The Law and Practical Issues' by Melissa Stock

'A Practical Guide to Planning Law and Rights of Way in National Parks, the Broads and AONBs' by James Maurici QC, James Neill et al

'A Practical Guide to Election Law' by Tom Tabori

'A Practical Guide to the Law in Relation to Surrogacy' by Andrew Powell

'A Practical Guide to Claims Arising from Fatal Accidents – Second Edition' by James Patience

'A Practical Guide to Asbestos Claims' by Jonathan Owen & Gareth McAloon

'A Practical Guide to Stamp Duty Land Tax in England and Northern Ireland' by Suzanne O'Hara

'A Practical Guide to the Law of Farming Partnerships' by Philip Whitcomb

'A Practical Guide to the Law of Unlawful Eviction and Harassment – Second Edition' by Stephanie Lovegrove

'A Practical Guide to Costs in Personal Injury Claims – Second Edition' by Matthew Hoe

'A Practical Guide to the General Data Protection Regulation (GDPR) – Second Edition' by Keith Markham

'A Practical Guide to Working with Litigants in Person and McKenzie Friends in Family Cases' by Stuart Barlow

'Protecting Unregistered Brands: A Practical Guide to the Law of Passing Off' by Lorna Brazell

'A Practical Guide to Secondary Liability and Joint Enterprise Post-Jogee' by Joanne Cecil & James Mehigan

'A Practical Guide to the Pre-Action RTA Claims Protocol for Personal Injury Lawyers' by Antonia Ford

'A Practical Guide to Neighbour Disputes and the Law' by Alexander Walsh

'A Practical Guide to Coercive Control for Legal Practitioners and Victims' by Rachel Horman

'A Practical Guide to the Law of Driverless Cars – Second Edition'

by Alex Glassbrook, Emma Northey & Scarlett Milligan

'A Practical Guide to TOLATA Claims' by Greg Williams

'A Practical Guide to Elderly Law – Second Edition' by Justin Patten

'A Practical Guide to Responding to Housing Disrepair and Unfitness Claims' by Iain Wightwick

'A Practical Guide to the Law of Bullying and Harassment in the Workplace' by Philip Hyland

'How to Be a Freelance Solicitor: A Practical Guide to the SRA-Regulated Freelance Solicitor Model' by Paul Bennett

'A Practical Guide to Prison Injury Claims' by Malcolm Johnson

'A Practical Guide to Advising Clients at the Police Station' by Colin Stephen McKeown-Beaumont

'A Practical Guide to Antisocial Behaviour Injunctions – Second Edition' by Iain Wightwick

'Practical Mediation: A Guide for Mediators, Advocates, Advisers, Lawyers, and Students in Civil, Commercial, Business, Property, Workplace, and Employment Cases' by Jonathan Dingle with John Sephton

'The Mini-Pupillage Workbook' by David Boyle

'A Practical Guide to Crofting Law' by Brian Inkster

'A Practical Guide to the Law of Domain Names and Cybersquatting' by Andrew Clemson

'A Practical Guide to the Law of Gender Pay Gap Reporting' by Harini Iyengar

'NHS Whistleblowing and the Law' by Joseph England

'Employment Law and the Gig Economy' by Nigel Mackay & Annie Powell

'A Practical Guide to Noise Induced Hearing Loss (NIHL) Claims' by Andrew Mckie, Ian Skeate, Gareth McAloon

'An Introduction to Beauty Negligence Claims – A Practical Guide for the Personal Injury Practitioner' by Greg Almond

'Intercompany Agreements for Transfer Pricing Compliance' by Paul Sutton

'Zen and the Art of Mediation' by Martin Plowman

'A Practical Guide to Adoption for Family Lawyers' by Graham Pegg

'A Practical Guide to Industrial Disease Claims' by Andrew Mckie & Ian Skeate

'A Practical Guide to Conducting a Sheriff Court Proof' by Andrew Stevenson

'A Practical Guide to Vicarious Liability' by Mariel Irvine

'A Practical Guide to Applications for Landlord's Consent and Variation of Leases' by Mark Shelton

'A Practical Guide to Relief from Sanctions Post-Mitchell and Denton' by Peter Causton

'A Practical Guide to Equity Release for Advisors' by Paul Sams

'A Practical Guide to Financial Services Claims' by Chris Hegarty

'A Practical Guide to Financial Ombudsman Service Claims' by Adam Temple & Robert Scrivenor

'A Practical Guide to Running Housing Disrepair and Cavity Wall Claims – Second Edition' by Andrew Mckie & Ian Skeate

'A Practical Guide to Holiday Sickness Claims – Second Edition' by Andrew Mckie & Ian Skeate

'Arguments and Tactics for Personal Injury and Clinical Negligence Claims' by Dorian Williams

'A Practical Guide to Drone Law' by Rufus Ballaster, Andrew Firman, Eleanor Clot

'On Experts: CPR35 for Lawyers and Experts' by David Boyle

'An Introduction to Personal Injury Law' by David Boyle

These books and more are available to order online direct from the publisher at www.lawbriefpublishing.com, where you can also read free sample chapters. For any queries, call us on 0844 587 2383 or email us at mail@lawbriefpublishing.com.

Our books are all generally in stock at www.amazon.co.uk with free next day delivery for Prime members, and at good legal bookshops such as Wildy & Sons.

We are regularly launching new books in our series of practical day-to-day practitioners' guides. Visit our website and join our free newsletter to be kept informed and to receive special offers, free chapters, etc.

You can also follow us on Twitter at www.twitter.com/lawbriefpub.

www.ingramcontent.com/pod-product-compliance
Lightning Source LLC
LaVergne TN
LVHW050303210926
848481LV00014BA/818

9781918241068